Cuba

- A  in the text denotes a highly recommended sight
- A complete A–Z of practical information starts on p.104

Berlitz Publishing Company, Inc.

Princeton   Mexico City   Dublin   Eschborn   Singapore

Text:	Fred Mawer
Editors:	Donna Dailey, Peter Duncan
Photography:	Fred Mawer
Layout:	Media Content Marketing, Inc.
Cartography:	⊕ Falk-Verlag, Munich

Thanks to Cubana de Aviación, Interchange, Emily Hatchwell, and Tim Donovan for their help in the preparation of this guide.

Found an error we should know about? Our editor would be happy to hear from you, and a postcard would do. Although we make every effort to ensure the accuracy of all the information in this book, changes do occur.

ISBN 2-8315-6296-1
Revised 1998 – First Printing January 1998

Printed in Switzerland by Weber SA, Bienne
019/801 REV

CONTENTS

CUBA

CUBA AND THE CUBANS

Cuba, the largest island in the Caribbean, with a population of nearly 11 million, conjures up many idyllic images. Limpid, azure waters lap against palm-fringed sands. Cool, verdant courtyards lie within colonial buildings painted in dazzling colours. Slick barmen concoct exotic cocktails while weatherbeaten farmers puff on succulent seven-inch-long cigars. Sensational salsa bands play late into the night, and rubber-hipped dancers jive to Latin rhythms.

For many visitors, Cuba is exactly this hedonistic playground, and a relatively inexpensive one at that. Yet, as one of the last bastions of Communism in the world — or put another way, as the last place in the Western Hemisphere without a McDonald's — there is a great deal more to this complicated nation.

Cuba is a highly politicized country. Everywhere you go, giant billboards exhort people to greater things. A common rallying cry is the unequivocal *socialismo o muerte* (socialism or death), while portraits of Che Guevara, the 1960s Marxist martyr, and Fidel Castro, still Cuban president after almost 40 years, can be seen in shops, offices, and homes.

Politics infiltrate almost all aspects of life. Children are sworn in at the age of six to become Communist Pioneers. Christmas has been abolished. On every block you'll see a sign for a CDR, a Committee for the Defense of the Revolution, whose purpose is to keep tabs on any murmurings of discontent and ensure that everyone is pulling his or her weight within the community.

The revolution which took place in 1959 has undoubtedly brought about social achievements that would be worthy of

Pleasure boaters come ashore to enjoy both the sun and shade of Cuba's idyllic beaches.

praise in First World countries, let alone undeveloped nations. Average life expectancy rose from 57 years in 1958 to 75 in 1992; the number of people per doctor decreased from 5,000 in 1958 to 400 in 1988; literacy rates improved from 76 percent of the population in 1958 to 95 percent in 1992. Crime is enviably low, and the bubbliness of schoolchildren, all dressed in maroon or mustard-coloured uniforms, is a joy to behold.

So what's the downside? There's no freedom of speech, freedom of the press, freedom to travel outside the country, and there's only one political party. Everything has always creaked and stuttered in hard-pressed Communist Cuba, but now that it's no longer bolstered by an empathetic Soviet Union, its people are really suffering. Although there are few outright beggars, everyone is hungry: government rations simply don't suffice. Families often live in appallingly over-crowded conditions, so couples seeking privacy rent out rooms in posadas or "love hotels" by the hour. Buses are ancient, and fuel shortages mean there are far too few on the roads. Travelling and buying food usually require standing for ages in *la cola* (the queue, or line): Cubans think nothing of waiting a couple of hours just for an ice-cream, or half a day for a bus.

Tourist Dollars

In their smart hotels and air-conditioned buses, tourists are insulated from such hardships. As Cuba is in desperate need of hard currency, it's promoting tourism aggressively. Compared with less than a quarter of a million holiday makers in 1985, the numbers now exceed one million, making tourism the country's second-most-important source of revenue after the sugar industry.

With official monthly salaries paid in the local currency and worth just a few dollars on the all-important black market, a large number of Cubans understandably look to benefit in some way from their relatively wealthy visi-

A Havana billboard urging citizens to "defend happiness" signals hard times.

Cuban Highlights

Places

Havana. Cuba's capital, at turns vibrant, decrepit, puzzling, but always sensationally beautiful. (See page 26)

Viñales Valley. Scenic tobacco country. (See page 49)

Trinidad. Cuba's most enchanting town, with cobblestone streets and glorious colonial buildings. (See page 61)

Santiago de Cuba. The second-largest city, more laid-back than Havana, and renowned for its music. (See page 75)

Baracoa. An exquisite town, the first founded in Cuba. (See page 81)

Experiences

A top cabaret. These colourful extravaganzas are not everyone's cup of tea, but worth experiencing. (See page 89)

A casa de la trova. Small Cuban bands play music for free, often in lovely colonial buildings. (See page 92)

A tobacco factory. See cigars being made. (See pages 40, 48)

A haircut and shave. Old-fashioned barbers are two-a-penny. Women can have their nails trimmed or painted.(See page 39)

Visiting a person's home. To see how Cubans live, take up one of the many invitations you'll receive. (See page 96)

Scuba diving. Excellent coral life. (See page 86)

Cuba's top resorts

Varadero. Cuba's biggest, brashest resort by far. First-rate hotels, a fabulous beach, and decent nightlife, though little charm. (See page 53)

Playa Santa Lucía. Isolated hotels strung along a fine beach. Excursions to offshore cays. (See page 69)

Cayo Coco and Cayo Guillermo. Presently just one good hotel on each cay. Great beaches, plane trips. (See page 66)

Cayo Largo. A resort island with fine beaches and boat trips to local cays, little local life. (See page 50)

Guardalavaca. Hotels alongside a lovely beach. Gorgeous, lush countryside all around. (See page 71) tors. Attempts at sightseeing frequently come to a grinding halt as locals seek to attract your attention.

A minority, who make an income by way of shady tourist dealings, are known as the *jineteros/jineteras*, literally "jockeys," trying to hitch a ride on the back of visitors.

A Joyful Spirit

A joke in Havana goes that an official United Nations survey asks citizens round the world whether they have any opinions on poverty in their country. From Japan to Argentina, the common response comes, "We have no poverty here"; in Cuba, the reply is, "We have no opinions here."

Cuba's vivacious children usually appear immune from their country's hardships.

Yet despite the dangers of speaking out, numerous Cubans want to tell you of their desire to travel abroad, of the trials of their day-to-day existence, of what they think of their great leader. Many will condemn the tourism apartheid and the fact that those who can acquire dollars can live well: it's divisive, they argue, and anathema in a socialist state. Some put the country's troubles down to economic incompetence, others to the United States, and its refusal to trade.

In spite of all these tribulations, the unbelievably joyful Cuban spirit is undimmed. Cubans are incredibly gregarious and hospitable, inviting you into their homes given half a chance. They are wonderfully tactile: lots of hand-shaking, shoulder clasping, and kissing is in order in any encounter.

Wherever you are in Cuba, from restaurants to airport departure lounges, from central squares to dusty back-streets, someone is always playing a tune, someone is ready to dance, and someone is always chatting up someone else. Cubans are spontaneous and, moreover, laudably resourceful: children amuse themselves with improvised skateboards and kites, while adults tinker away at car engines, somehow managing to keep the country's extensive vintage fleet of 1950s vehicles more or less on the road.

Some parts of Cuba still live in a different decade. Havana's airport is nick-named "the time machine": you step back into the past the moment you arrive, as you are greeted by scenes of oxen ploughing the fields and horses and traps plying the streets. Then you head back to the present when you leave.

Vintage vehicles and drive-in dining may give visitors a sense of going back in time.

HISTORY

When Christopher Columbus landed in eastern Cuba on 27 October 1492, he did the Cuban tourist authorities an everlasting favour by writing that the land was "the most lovely that eyes have ever seen." He didn't realize Cuba was an island, believing that he'd found the empire of the Great Khan in Asia.

Indian tribes such as the Siboney from Central and South America had lived on the island since at least as long ago as 1000 B.C., but when Columbus arrived the most important group were the Taíno. They were a relatively sophisticated and unbelligerent people who cultivated crops, including tobacco, and lived in *bohíos*, or thatched huts, much like those still seen in rural Cuba today.

The Spanish conquest of the island was delayed until 1511, when Diego Velázquez sailed from neighbouring Hispaniola with some 300 *conquistadores* (conquerors). Baracoa was the first of seven settlements. Indians were enslaved and in the process exposed to European diseases. Whole villages committed suicide, and by the mid-1550s the Indian population had dropped from over 100,000 to 3,000.

A statue of Columbus in Baracoa—locals claim he disembarked here in 1492.

Piracy and Trade

Cuba remained an insignificant colony, but by the end of the 16th century, thanks to its strategic position in the Gulf of Mexico, it had become a naval base for Spain's fleets travelling between Europe and her colonies. Ports like Havana and Santiago de Cuba were heavily fortified, since French and English pirate raids were common. A great trade in contraband operated from bases around the island, too.

Oxen pulling carts are still a very common sight throughout the country.

In 1762, British forces captured Havana. They only held it for a year, before returning it to Spain in exchange for Florida, but during this period Cuba had a brief taste of things to come, as trade was temporarily opened up to countries other than Spain, notably the American colonies.

The country had long been developing a lucrative tobacco industry, and after 1763 the expanding sugar-cane business took off, with the importation of hundreds of thousands of African slaves to carry out the labour-intensive work. Shortly after, Cuba took over the mantle of the Caribbean's principal sugar producer from Hispaniola, whose own sugar industry collapsed as the result of a slave revolt which led to the creation of Haiti.

By the middle of the 19th century Cuba was one of the most valuable colonies in the world, producing a quarter of the world's sugar, with half a million slaves (nearly half the population) and at least 3,500 trading ships visiting per year.

The Road to Independence

The ruling class in Cuba was made up of people born in Spain (*peninsulares*) and appointed to office by the Spanish crown. Spaniards born and raised in Cuba were known as *criollos* (creoles). They managed the sugar-cane plantations but were not involved in the running of the country. During the 19th century some *criollos*, particularly in Oriente, the island's poorer eastern end, became increasingly disenchanted with their lot. Heavy Spanish taxes deprived them of potential wealth, and the abolition of slavery in the United States as a result of the American Civil War meant an imminent end to their cheap source of manpower.

On 10 October 1868, Carlos Manuel de Céspedes, a *criollo* plantation owner who had already played a brief part in uprisings in Spain, issued a call for independence and liberated his slaves from his estate, La Demajagua. After early signs of success, his movement was countered by heavy troop reinforcements from Spain. During the subsequent Ten Years' War—fought by rebels under the now greatly revered generals Máximo Gómez, Calixto García, and Antonio Maceo—50,000 Cubans, including Céspedes, and more than 200,000 Spanish lost their lives. Cuba remained Spanish but the war contributed to the abolition of slavery on the island and fostered a national consciousness.

An ancient fortification at Santiago's Morro Castle, built in the 16th century.

The next important uprising against Spain came in 1895, at the instigation of José Martí, Cuba's most venerated patriot (who now has a street, square, or building named after him in every town). Born in 1853, he was exiled at the age of 18 for his political views, then led a career in journalism, mainly in the United States, in which he gave eloquent voice to Cuban independence and fleshed out concepts of justice and equality for the people.

Martí was soon killed, and leadership during the War of Independence passed to generals Gómez and Maceo. Again, the war brought about great destruction, notably of sugar mills and cane fields, as well as enormous bloodshed: some 300,000 Cubans died.

Throughout the 19th century the United States had become increasingly involved in Cuban affairs, partly because of the island's geographic significance, partly through financial dominance of its sugar market. A U.S. purchase of the island from Spain had long been on the agenda, and many Cubans saw annexation as a positive step towards independence, even though Martí had stressed that Cuba should beware of becoming a satellite of the United States ("I know the Monster, because I have lived in its lair," he wrote).

The Maceo monument in Santiago recalls the Ten Years' War.

In February 1898, the *U.S.S. Maine* was sunk in Havana's harbour, killing all 260 crew members. Spanish responsibility was never incontrovertibly established, but the United States used the sinking as a pretext to declare war. U.S. victory came swiftly, with Spain surrendering claim to the island by the end of the same year. A provisional military government lasted through to 1902, when Cuba became an independent republic under its first president, Tomás Estrada Palma.

Colonial architecture greets you at every turn round the island—this is in Central Havana.

False Independence

For the next five decades the United States dominated Cuba's economy and largely controlled its political processes. In 1901, the Platt Amendment formally established limited U.S. authority over the island by allowing intervention for "the preservation of Cuban independence," and by 1906 the United States had installed a temporary military-backed government.

The period was also characterized by political corruption, violence, and terrorism. Two infamous personalities rose to prominence. General Gerardo Machado was democratically elected president in 1924 but soon instituted a dictatorship, censoring the press, banning public meetings, and assassinating opponents. From 1933 Fulgencio Batista, though only a sergeant, held the strings of power through a series of puppet presidents, before winning the presidency for himself in 1940. He retired in 1944, but staged an easily achieved military coup in 1952. His venal dictatorship made it possible for him to invest some $300 million abroad by 1959.

Since the 1920s, disillusionment with the fledgling republic—with its clear dependence on the United States and its lack of political probity or social equality—had been steadily growing. Although Cuba had the second-highest per capita income in Latin America, prosperity did not filter down to the poor (in 1950, the World Bank adjudged 40 to 60 percent of Cubans to be undernourished). In Havana there was a greater concentration of dollar millionaires than anywhere else in Central or South America, and the capital was dubbed "an offshore Las Vegas" for its brothels, casinos, and gangsters.

The Road to Revolution

On 26 July 1953, rebels attacked the Moncada Barracks (the country's second most important military base) in Santiago de Cuba. The assault was an outright failure, but it thrust into the limelight its leader, Fidel Castro. Castro was taken prisoner and put on trial; his two-hour-long defense speech, later published as *History Will Absolve Me*, became a seminal revolutionary manifesto. Castro was incarcerated on the Isle of Pines (now called the Isle of Youth) until May 1955, when Batista granted an amnesty to political prisoners.

Castro went to Mexico. The following year he returned to southeastern Cuba with a force of 81 guerrillas, including Che Guevara (see page 21), crammed onto a small pleasure cruiser, the *Granma*. Only 15 reached the safety of the Sierra Maestra mountains. Miraculously, from such inauspicious beginnings, with the help of local peasants who were promised land reform, the so-called 26 of July Movement grew into a serious guerrilla army.

While Castro's forces sabotaged factories and skirmished with Batista's troops, the dictator did himself no favours by killing and torturing those suspected of rebel collusion. Following a disastrous offensive by government troops on the rebels' mountain strongholds in 1958, on 1 January 1959 Batista fled the country for the Dominican Republic, and the *barbudos* (the bearded ones) triumphantly entered Santiago, then Havana one week later.

Castro's Cuba

Immediately, rents were reduced, new wage levels were set, and estates were limited in size to 1,000 acres. A full nationalization programme followed, with the expropriation of factories, utilities, and more land. By the end of the 1960s, nearly everyone was employed by the state. At the same time, enlightened programmes were set in place to eradicate illiteracy and provide free universal schooling and health care.

Not everyone was pleased by the new arrangements. The media was soon placed under state control, and Committees for the Defense of the Revolution (CDRs) were established to keep tabs on dissenters. In the early years, tens of thousands of people suspected of being unsympathetic were detained, imprisoned, or sent to labour camps, along with other "undesirable" people, such as homosexuals and priests.

Che Guevara, the 1960s icon for left-wing romantics the world over.

Between 1959 and 1962 approximately 200,000 Cubans, mainly professionals and the better off, left the country. This began a pattern of settlement for expatriate Cubans in nearby Florida; a further 200,000 went in the Freedom Flights Programme between 1965 and 1971, and 125,000 followed in 1980

Che and Fidel

Ernesto "Che" Guevara (*che* meaning "mate" or "buddy") is the untainted personification of the Cuban revolution, idolized by Cubans and even eulogized daily by five-year-old schoolchildren who begin classes chanting "We will be like Che!"

Born in 1928 in Argentina, Che trained as a doctor before becoming a nomadic soul in South and Central America with a pile of Marxist literature in his rucksack. He met Castro in Mexico in 1955, and for the next ten years was Castro's right-hand man, as a guerrilla in the mountains, then as director of the national bank (signing bills just "Che"), minister of industry, and minister of the economy.

Che's idealistic view of the *Hombre Nuevo* (New Man) who seeks no personal gain, and his insistence on ultra-centralization, did great harm to Cuba's economy in the 1960s. In 1965, he left Cuba for new causes — which deserved the "staccato singing of the machine guns and the new battle cries of war and victory"—and was killed trying to foment revolt in Bolivia in 1967.

Fidel Castro—president of the country, secretary-general of the Communist Party, and commander-in-chief of the armed forces—was born in 1927 and trained as a lawyer at the University of Havana. Commonly just called Fidel, he also bears a host of nicknames: "the horse," "the air hostess" (he's always asking Cubans to tighten their belts), and "the bearded one" (sometimes people just stroke their chins to refer to him).

Once a puritanical guerrilla fighter and always a consummate demagogue, he can talk articulately without notes from a platform for hours. His personality and longevity in power dwarf that of most other world leaders. He has, in fact, outlasted eight American presidents, despite many reputed CIA assassination attempts that have included exploding cigars.

A billboard at the Bay of Pigs translates as, "The first defeat of imperialism in Latin America."

when Castro lifted travel restrictions from the port of Mariel (west of Havana).

According to official Washington estimates, U.S. businesses lost $8 billion through the nationalization programme, in seized assets such as Cuba's telephone and electricity companies, dozens of sugar mills, and hundreds of thousands of acres of land. In retaliation, in 1960 the U.S. government began a trade embargo against Cuba (called a blockade by the Cubans) which continues to this day. Furthermore, in 1961 CIA-trained Cuban exiles attempted to overthrow Castro's regime during the Bay of Pigs fiasco.

Washington was deeply unhappy with the way Cuba was evolving politically. Soon after the Bay of Pigs, Castro declared himself a Marxist-Leninist. (In 1976 the Communist Party was formally established as the country's only permissable political organization.) As Castro had not displayed any Communist inclinations in the 1950s, some suggest that he adopted his new political mantle to ingratiate himself with the Soviet Union. In 1960, the two countries began swapping oil for sugar; by the end of the 1980s, more than 80 per cent of all Cuba's trade was conducted with the USSR, which also provided Cuba with a subsidy worth an estimated annual $5 billion.

In 1962, Soviet president Nikita Khrushchev installed 42 medium-range nuclear missiles in Cuba. Once their presence was discovered, U.S. president John F. Kennedy imposed a naval quarantine on the island to ensure no more missiles arrived, and insisted that the existing ones had to go. After six days, the crisis came to an end when Khrushchev gave way, in return for a U.S. promise never to invade Cuba.

The Special Period

Soviet trade and subsidy were crucial factors in propping up Cuba's heavily centralized and often badly planned economy until the end of the 1980s. But democratization across Eastern Europe and the break-up of the Soviet Union suddenly left Cuba bereft of food, oil, and hard currency.

The government announced the start of a "Special Period in Peacetime" in 1990 and introduced new austerity measures. Though rationing had existed since the early 1960s, it has been increased to cover many more items, with the result that it has become virtually impossible for Cubans to live on rations alone. Power cuts bring factories and whole cities to a standstill, while sugar cane is left to rot in the fields as there is no machinery to harvest it. The bicycle and horse and cart have become preferred forms of transport. To make matters worse, in 1992 the Cuba Democracy Act extended the U.S. embargo to cover a ban on trade with Cuba for foreign subsidiaries of U.S. companies.

As in Communist Vietnam, in order to survive, the government is introducing a limited number of capitalist measures while maintaining a firm political grip. Foreign investment in joint ventures with Cuban companies, in fields such as tourism and mineral and oil exploration, is keenly encouraged and is

A Cuban soldier looks over Guantánamo Bay Naval Base from a raised bunker.

being taken up by Canadian, Mexican, and Spanish firms. The possibility of moral corruption from the expanding tourism industry is seen as a necessary evil as it brings in so much hard currency. Most Cubans would agree that, with measures such as the legalization of the dollar and small-scale private enterprises in 1993, and the introduction of private farmers' markets in 1994, their welfare has perceptibly improved.

Yet in Havana there were serious anti-government riots during the summer of 1994, and many Cubans would emigrate if they could. In August 1994, Castro suddenly lifted restrictions on those wishing to leave (normally coastal patrols force potential emigrées to return). More than 30,000 Cubans tried to make it across to Florida on improvised rafts constructed of cork, tires, and wood. Many drowned or were eaten by sharks, and facing such numbers President Clinton abolished the U.S. policy of automatic asylum to Cuban refugees, placing them in a makeshift tent settlement in Guantánamo Bay Naval Base (see page 80).

The outdated and isolated socialist dinosaur that is Cuba soldiers on against all odds. The U.S. embargo, denounced by an ever-increasing majority in the United Nations (in 1994, by 101 votes to 2, with 48 abstentions), is intended largely as a punishment for this anti-democratic regime. Yet ironically, only the lifting of these trade sanctions may herald the end of Communist Cuba, as the island may then be swamped by unadulterated commercialism.

Historical Landmarks

1492   Christopher Columbus discovers Cuba.

1511   Diego Velázquez begins Spanish settlement.

1519   Founding of Havana on its present site.

1762   British forces seize Havana and remain for a year.

1868–78   Ten Years' War for Cuban independence; brought to an end by Spanish victory.

1886   End of slavery in Cuba.

1895   War of Independence begins; José Martí killed.

1898   Sinking of the *U.S.S. Maine*; United States declares war on Spain and wins; Spain surrenders Cuba.

1901   Platt Amendment legitimizes ongoing American involvement in Cuba.

1902   Formation of the Republic of Cuba.

1934   Platt Amendment annulled.

1940–44   Fulgencio Batista rules as president.

1952   Batista resumes power in military coup.

1953   Fidel Castro launches failed attack on the Moncada Barracks (26 July).

1956   Castro returns to Cuba on the yacht *Granma* and begins guerrilla operations.

1959   Castro seizes power (1 Jan); Batista flees the country.

1961   CIA-trained Cuban exiles defeated at the Bay of Pigs.

1962   Cuban Missile Crisis.

1980   125,000 Cubans leave Cuba from the port of Mariel.

1990   Soviet trade and subsidies disappear; new austerity measures of Special Period begin.

1993   Economic reforms begin, including acceptance of U.S. dollars as currency in Cuba.

1994   Exodus of 30,000 rafters for Florida; most were returned to Guantánamo Bay Naval Base.

1995   More reforms include sale of real estate to foreigners; open markets, in which farmers are allowed to sell food directly to consumers, proliferate.

WHERE TO GO

Nicolás Guillén, the nation's finest poet, described Cuba as a "long green alligator." Long it certainly is — 1,250 km (776 miles) from snout to tail. Almost the size of England, the island is divided into 14 provinces (established as replacements for the three provinces that existed before the revolution) and incorporates some 1,500 offshore islands, known as *cayos*, or cays.

Given its size, you would need at least a month to explore Cuba fully. This guide begins in the capital Havana, then heads down to the prized tobacco lands in the west, before doubling back across the plains of sugar cane in central Cuba to the soaring mountains in the east. Every region has charming, fascinating towns, and resort hotels beside quintessential Caribbean beaches are dotted round the whole island. However, you will find Cuba is simply too beguiling to spend your whole holiday roasting on the beach.

HAVANA (LA HABANA)

The island's capital, with almost 3 million inhabitants, is one of the most intoxicating cities in the world. Ever since its early maritime days and through to the 1950s when the gangsters who ran prostitution and gambling rackets made Havana a byword for decadence, it has always held a seedy allure. During the 19th century travellers described it as "wonderful, quaint, and beautiful" and "villainously odiferous," and both epithets still apply today: fetid backstreets sit side by side with squares ensconced among magnificently restored colonial buildings.

The country's present economic woes give Havana a languorous air and only a toe-hold on the late 20th century. It wakes up to the sound of the cockerel rather than the automobile, and its inhabitants, *habaneros*, while away the hours framed photogenically in shadowy doorways and on crumbling balconies.

Old Havana (La Habana Vieja)

Havana was established here in 1519 because of its vast natural harbour. During the 16th century a fleet of galleons laden with treasures annually used the port as a pit-stop on the way back to Spain from the New World. By the 17th century constant pirate attacks had resulted in extensive city defenses — colossal forts, a chain across the harbour mouth, and prominent city walls — making Havana the "Bulwark of the West Indies."

Vedado's skyscape provides a dramatic backdrop to the Malecón, Havana's waterfront roadway.

The richest residents lived with their slaves in grand mansions constructed in *mudéjar* style, a Christian/Moslem architectural tradition evolved in Spain. Behind massive doors, slatted blinds, carved window bars called *rejas*, and half-moon stained-glass windows known as *mediopuntos* lurked hidden courtyards bathed in penumbral light.

On account of these architectural wonders UNESCO declared Old Havana a World Heritage Site in 1982. A small number of buildings have been spruced up, but many others are propped up by wooden poles — their arcades, fluted pillars, and mosaic tiles on their last legs. This picturesque delapidation blends into dusty backstreets that assault the nose with a tropical cocktail of urine, cigars, and coffee and the ears with the ting-a-lings of bicycles, foghorns from the distant harbour, and coaxing Latin rhythms from nearby tenements. Scrawny cats and dogs roam the streets, a granny on a balcony hauls up her shopping in a bucket on a rope, and at night the streets are pitch dark except for the neon glow of TV sets from tiny front rooms.

Plaza de Armas

Old Havana can only be experienced on foot. The natural place to start a tour is at the city's oldest square, the **Plaza de Armas**, centred around a statue of the patriot Céspedes and encompassed by shaded marble benches and second-hand booksellers.

> When visiting churches: shorts, backless dresses, and tank tops should not be worn.

On the square's eastern side the small neoclassical temple, **El Templete**, marks the spot where the first Mass was said in 1519. The squat, moated **Castillo de la Real Fuerza** (Castle of the Royal Forces), to the north, begun in 1558, is one of the oldest forts in the Americas. It holds

Havana Highlights

Exploring

Plaza de Armas, Plaza de la Catedral. Old Havana's two show-piece squares, in glorious colonial buildings. (See pages 28, 30)

Calles Obispo, O'Reilly, Obra Pía. Old Havana's atmospheric principal thoroughfares. (See pages 32, 33)

Prado. A tree-lined boulevard teeming with Cuban life and lined with dazzling, faded architecture. (See page 36)

Malecón. The splendid yet down-at-heel seafront. (See page 39)

Museums and sights

Casa Museo de Ernest Hemingway. Hemingway's house, full of original furnishings and possessions. Mon and Wed-Sat 9am-4pm, Sun 9am-noon; closed if raining. (See page 43)

Cementerio de Cristóbal Colón. A colossal cemetery dating from 1868, with many over-the-top mausoleums. (See page 42)

Museo de la Revolución. A full account of Cuba's revolution, in the presidential palace. Sat 1pm-6pm, Sun 10am-1pm. (See page 37)

Morro and Cabaña castles. Great city views from vast colonial strongholds. Tues-Sat 10am-6pm and Sun 9am-1pm and Thurs-Mon 10 am-6pm. (See page 38)

Palacio de los Capitanes Generales. The city's museum in a Baroque palace. Daily 9.30am-6.30pm. (See page 30)

Partagas tobacco factory. A massive working cigar factory. Tours Mon-Fri and every other Sat 9am and 2pm. (See page 40)

Eating, drinking, and nightlife

La Bodeguita del Medio. Renowned for graffiti and splendid *mojitos* (cocktails). (See pages 32 and 139.)

El Floridita. Famous for well-documented Hemingway connections and daiquiris. (See pages 32 and 140)

El Patio. The city's finest courtyard dining-room. (See page 140)

Hotel Riviera. The best salsa and jazz in town. (See page 92)

Sevilla and Nacional hotels. Havana's plushest. (See page 131)

Tropicana. Famous open-air cabaret. (See page 90)

modern art exhibitions downstairs, and the battlements afford good views over the harbour. Look out for the *La Giraldilla* weather vane on a tower. The woman scanning the seas for her lost governor husband is the symbol of the city and of Havana Club rum.

In 1791, the seat of government and governor's (or captain general's) residence was transferred from the fort to the newly built Baroque **Palacio de los Capitanes Generales** (Palace of the Captain Generals) on the square's western flank. The presidential palace and then the municipal palace until Castro seized power, it is now **Museo de la Ciudad de la Habana** (the Museum of the City of Havana). Beyond the serene courtyard and its statue of Columbus lie a succession of splendid marbled and chandeliered rooms, some housing old cannonballs and coaches, others decked out in gilded furnishings. The most hallowed room commemorates Cuba's 19th-century independence wars, with the very first Cuban flag and venerated personal objects from generals of the day. The street surface outside is wooden, explained, some say, by the fact that a governor complained that carriages rattling on the cobbles kept him awake at night.

A statue of Manuel de Céspedes stands over Plaza de Armas.

Plaza de la Catedral

Plaza de la Catedral is so lovely it could be a stage set.

Balcony life—local residents soak up the sun in this classic scene of Old Havana.

Most days a colourful crafts market spreads across the cobbled square, distracting from the superb colonial mansions with their bright shutters and *mediopuntos*, and the glorious wavy Baroque façade and asymmetrical towers of the late-18th-century church. The cathedral's interior, usually open only on Sunday mornings, is plainer than you'd expect.

Of particular interest here is the **Museo de Arte Colonial**, in a fine palace constructed in 1720. Its yellow courtyard and little-altered architectural features are complemented by a large collection of 17th- and 18th-century furniture.

Another mansion, Casa de Lombillo, houses the **Museo de la Educación**. Its most interesting displays publicize the successful *Campaña de la Alfabetización* (literacy campaign) conducted in the early years of the revolution. Opposite the museum, be sure to at least peek at the breathtaking courtyard of El Patio restaurant (see page 140).

Just round the corner on Calle Empedrado, you'll find the restaurant **La Bodeguita del Medio** (see page 139), as well as art exhibitions in the **Centro Cultural Wilfredo Lam**, named after Cuba's top modern artist. Books, manuscripts, and photographs of the country's best-known novelist are housed inside the **Centro de Promoción Cultural Alejo Carpentier**.

Even the modest produce stands are picturesque in Old Havana.

Around Calle Obispo

Connecting Plaza de Armas with the Parque Central, **Calle Obispo** is Old Havana's most important and smartest thoroughfare, pedestrianized with missile heads as bollards. Here you can peer into chemists' shops that have not changed since the 19th century. Equally fascinating are the two parallel, partly residential streets, O'Reilly and Obrapía, where grand Neoclassical and colonial buildings intermingle with decrepit tenements.

Much of restored Old Havana is concentrated in a few blocks at the eastern end of these streets. The museums in the vicinity are worth visiting as much for their glorious colonial mansions as for their contents. Starting from Plaza de Armas, head down Calle Oficios. Just on the right, the **Museo Numismático** has a comprehensive set of Cuban coins and banknotes. A little farther on lies the

Casa de los Arabes, whose 17th-century building now serves as a souk piled high with carpets, robes, and pottery, a place of worship for Moslems, and a restaurant (see page 140).

Turn right into Calle Obrapía. On the corner of Calle Mercaderes, the creamy **Casa de la Obra Pía** is a real 17th-century architectural wonder, with Baroque additions around a flower-drenched courtyard and a full set of beautifully furnished domestic rooms.

The massive mansion opposite is nearly as impressive and houses the **Casa de Africa**. There are pelts, drums, costumes, carved figures, and furniture from some 26 African countries, as well as a tantalizingly interesting Santería (see page 35) collection.

Most days you can find the Plaza de la Catedral bustling with a colourful crafts market.

Turning up Mercaderes, you will soon come to the **Casa de Puerto Rico** (also called the Casa de Tabaco) on the left. Its small collection of smoking-related objects include lighters shaped as a piano, typewriter, camera, and telephone; the building is also home to the Cuban Language Academy.

On the corner of Mercaderes and Obispo is the **Hotel Ambos Mundos**. If ongoing renovations allow it, visit Room 511, arranged with original artifacts from Hemingway's sojourns here in the 1930s. Those with the Hemingway bug should go to **El Floridita** (see page 140) at the western end of Calle Obispo. The writer immortalized the swanky bar in *Islands in the Stream*. Hemingway photos adorn the walls, his seat is on the extreme left of the bar as you enter, and his favourite daiquiri is now called Papa Hemingway, with double rum and no sugar (the barmen claim he was diabetic).

Plaza Vieja and Around

The aptly named **Plaza Vieja** (Old Square) began life around 1584 as a place where wealthy merchants lived. Most of its mansions are now in a very sorry state, but they are slowly being restored to something of their former glory. On the southwest corner a fine 18th-century palace has been converted into an arts centre.

The old backstreets here are full of character, but are little visited by tourists, and care should be taken with possessions. On Calle Cuba between calles Amargura and Brasil, the **Museo Histórico de las Ciencias Carlos J. Finlay** is a marvellously fusty old place, with a domed lecture theatre, portrait gallery, library, and pharmacy.

Signs:
llegada / arrival
salida / departure

The Cult of the Gods

Santería, "the cult of the gods," came from the Yoruba people in Nigeria. It is estimated that up to 90 percent of Cubans have at some time practised its rituals — including, it is alleged, even Castro — and its popularity seems to be on the increase. There are hundreds of gods, called *orishas*, in the Santería pantheon, each with a specific character as in classical mythology. Worshippers affiliate themselves to a particular *orisha*, visibly through necklaces and shrines of propitiatory food and drink in their homes. Each *orisha* has a Catholic saint as a counterpart: slaves intermingled their religious practices with Catholicism so that they would go unhindered by the Spanish. Saints' days are celebrated with much Afro-Cuban drum beating and dancing.

The best place to learn about Santería in Guanabacoa, east of Havana harbour, is at Guanabacoa's historical museum. You can view the sanctum where a *babalawo* (high priest) performs divinations, a fundamental aspect of Santería. In Old Havana there's also a Santería exhibition in the Casa de Africa (see page 33), and a Santería shop (see page 85).

Once the Academy of Sciences, it is named after the Cuban who discovered that mosquitoes transmit yellow fever. Slightly farther down Calle Cuba between calles Sol and Luz stands the 17th-century **Convento de Santa Clara**, an expansive complex in varying states of disrepair, set round a tranquil courtyard garden full of exotic trees. A convent until 1919, it is now an architectural conservation centre.

By the train station on Calle Leonor Pérez between calles Picota and Egido is the modest **Casa Natal de José Martí** (Birthplace of José Martí). The numerous personal effects on display leave you in no doubt as to Martí's importance in the

The play of light and shadow lends Old Havana a mysterious aura.

pantheon of Cuban heroes. The station itself is fascinating, with hundreds of people waiting in line, and a parking lot full of rickshaw-style bicycles and Cadillac taxis.

The Prado and Around

Wide avenues skirt western Old Havana. The loveliest is the **Prado**, running from Parque Central to the sea. Sumptuous yet run-down buildings, with flamingo-pink and lime-green façades and ornate columns and balustrades, flank a raised boulevard of laurels, gas lamps, and marble benches. In the 19th century this was the fashionable place to promenade. Now it serves as a mini park for *habaneros*, from canoeing couples to children playing on homemade skateboards. In the giant stuccoed rooms of the **Gymnastics Academy** at number 207 on the Prado, muscular instructors put five-year-old prodigies through their paces on vaults and parallel bars.

On the palmy Parque Central, close by the handsome Inglaterra (see page 130), stands the magnificent **Gran Hotel Teatro**. The home of the national ballet school veritably drips with balustrades, shutters, and caryatids. The cavernous interior is hardly less awesome and on weekday tours you can even watch ballet rehearsals and lessons in progress.

Next along is the monumental **Capitolio**, a replica of the American capitol in Washington D.C. Completed in 1929, it symbolizes the time when the island was in the thrall of the United States. This former seat of government now houses the **Academy of Sciences**, including an educational science museum. Its vast bronze doors pictorially chart the island's history, and the immense main gallery inside has a diamond in the floor beneath the dome.

A trio of museums is strung along Zulueta, the avenue parallel to the Prado. The **Museo Nacional de Bellas Artes** (National Fine Arts Museum) has impressive collections of Egyptian, Greek, and Roman artifacts, as well as 16th- to 19th-century works of art by Europeans ranging from Canaletto to Turner; many of these pieces were taken from private collections after the revolution. However, the galleries are poorly lit, and you may find a number closed for restoration. Some rooms devoted to modern Cuban art have sensual pieces in Diego Rivera style, abstract creations by Wilfredo Lam, and post-revolutionary works as stimulating for their social comment as for their aesthetics.

Housed in the grand Presidential Palace used by presidents (and dictators) between 1920 and 1959, the **Museo de la Revolución** is the country's largest and most interesting museum; allow a couple of hours to view it. It presents an exhaustive view of all aspects of the revolution. The most absorbing sections chart the struggle to power, through countless maps, evocative photos of both torture victims and triumphal scenes, and assorted personal memorabilia from passports to bloodstained clothes. Documents accuse the CIA of introducing harmful viruses into Cuba. Cuttings from U.S. newspapers calling for an end to the trade embargo are prominently displayed, while thanks are offered to presidents Reagan and Bush, depicted as life-size cartoon versions of a sheriff and Roman emperor, for unintentionally cementing the revolution. In the square outside, the centrepiece is the ordinary-looking boat, the *Granma*, that carried Castro's 81 rebels in 1956. The bullet-pocked van marked "Fast Delivery" was used in a failed assassination of Batista in 1957.

On the seafront, the **Museo Nacional de la Música** (National Music Museum) is of interest mainly for its extensive, informative collection of African drums, and for its many stringed instruments.

The Capitolio looms over central Havana, home to the Partagas tobacco factory.

Two Castles

Cuba's most impressive castles sit brooding over the capital's commercial harbour. Take a taxi through the road tunnel underneath the water to reach them. The older one, constructed at the end of the 16th century, is the **Castillo de los Tres Santos Reyes Magos del Morro**, better known as Morro Castle. From its harbour-mouth position the views of Havana over the defiant cannons are magical.

The vast **Fortaleza de San Carlos de la Cabaña** (known as La Cabaña), running beside the harbour, was constructed after the English capture of Havana in 1763.

This is the largest fort ever built in the Americas. As well as being impressive and well preserved, the gardens and ramparts are romantically lit in the evening. A ceremony at 9:00 P.M. re-enacts the firing of a cannon which marked the closing of the city gates. A large exhibition covering the history of castles includes a reproduction battering ram and catapult.

New Havana

The walls of Old Havana disappeared during the 19th century to allow the city to expand westwards, which it now does in great grids of streets and avenues. The long, curvaceous **Malecón** (breakwater), a six-lane highway beside the seafront, links the districts of Central Havana and Vedado. At its eastern end, primary-coloured buildings gradually decay in tragic splendour. Havana's youth congregates here *en masse* on fine evenings, flying kites, swimming off the rocks, and setting out to sea in giant inner tubes to fish.

Central Havana

Central Havana (Centro Habana) is a tumbledown residential/commercial area. The city's main shopping street, **Calle San Rafael**, traverses it from the Parque Central westwards. While having a fascinating stroll here, you can stop to have your nails painted, or have a shave and a haircut, all right on the pavement. One of the country's new private mar-

When the sea is rough, waves crash over the Malecón's wall and onto the road.

Perks of the business — cigar rollers are allowed all the cigars they want.

kets has overrun Havana's small Chinatown, at calles Zanja and Rayo. The food on sale may be poor by Western standards, but free trade with plentiful supplies is an amazing sight in beleaguered Cuba.

The large **Partagas tobacco factory**, directly behind the Capitolio, is the biggest export factory in the country, with 200 rollers turning out 5 million cigars a year. This is the best factory to visit on the island, with an excellent shop. The rollers bang the table in unison to greet visitors (See page 48).

Vedado

Vedado's heyday was in the 1940s and 1950s, when gangsters such as Meyer Lansky held sway in the Nacional, Riviera, and Capri hotels. Stars like Frank Sinatra and Ginger Rogers performed, and American tourists spent their money in swanky casinos. The revolution put the lid on the nightlife, banning gambling and deporting the mafiosi.

Save for the highly ostentatious Nacional (see page 131), the hotels have now seen better days. Vedado is Havana's respectable business district, as well as being a leafy residential area, spacious and seemly in comparison with Old and Central Havana.

Business is centred on **La Rampa**, the name for Calle 23 from Calle L to the sea. Opposite the tower-block Hotel Habana Libre; the Havana Hilton in pre-revolutionary days, is the **Coppelia ice-cream park**. At this rather bizarre spot, locals queue literally for hours for the prized ice cream, eating many scoops in one sitting or ladling them into saucepans to take home. Hard-hearted foreigners can jump to the front of the line. A short walk up the hill brings you to the university, a quiet, attractive area of Neoclassical buildings. English-speaking students keen to meet foreigners are plentiful.

Directly east on Calle San Miguel between calles Ronda and Mazón is the fine **Museo Napoleónico**. This mansion is not only full of Empire furniture, but also houses a remarkable collection of Napoleonic memorabilia: busts, portraits, and even his pistol, hat, and death mask from St. Helena. The house and contents were acquired by the state from a rich owner in 1960, as was the **Museo de Artes Decorativas**, at Calle 17 between calles D and E. Each room in this grand 19th-century villa is furnished in a particular style: English

The Cementerio de Cristóbal Colón is undoubtedly Vedado's top sight, with its vast mausoleums and sea of marble.

Chippendale, Chinese, Baroque, or Art Deco in the fabulous bathroom.

Vedado's top sight is undoubtedly the **Cementerio de Cristóbal Colón** (Columbus Cemetery). A sea of creamy marble unfolds across this city of the dead, laid out in an enormous grid of streets. Vast mausoleums line the principal avenues of the cemetery. Cubans come to pray and place flowers at the tomb of La Milagrosa, "The Miracle Woman," who helps people in need. When leaving, they take care never to turn their backs on her.

Bizarre Havana: the Russian embassy building stands out in the suburb of Miramar.

Plaza de la Revolución

The soulless district known as **Plaza de la Revolución** is only worth visiting for a brief glimpse of the square of the same name, a vast concourse where political rallies are held. Hideous multi-storey ministry buildings erected in the 1950s by Batista and a giant, tapering concrete obelisk, looking like a rocket launch pad with a pensive José Martí at its foot, provide the scenery. Soldiers ask lingerers to move on.

Miramar

More attractive is the exclusive suburb of **Miramar** to the west. The villas of the pre-revolutionary wealthy have now been divided into apartments or turned into offices, but embassies still imbue the area with an upmarket feel. Drive along Avenida 5 to see them, each sporting a national flag.

At the corner of Calle 14, the **Museo del Ministerio del Interior** has some intriguing exhibits relating to CIA espionage, including code boxes concealed in briefcases, decoding equipment, and a transmitter hidden in a fake rock. Don't miss the Russian embassy, between calles 62 and 66, looking for all the world like an outsize concrete robot.

Just west on Avenida 3, the **diplomats' supermarket** may be drab by Western standards but is surely the best-stocked food hall in Cuba. Anyone with dollars can shop here. It's about the only place in Cuba where you can put together a picnic, which you could conceivably take to the antiseptic, modern **Hemingway Marina** a few miles west, which is usually peculiarly bereft of boats. It comes to life once a year for the Hemingway Marlin Fishing Tournament (see page 91).

Havana's Outskirts

Havana's suburbs are sprawling and grimy, but they contain a couple of places associated with Ernest Hemingway. From 1939 to 1960 the writer lived on and off in the Finca Vigía, now the **Casa Museo de Ernest Hemingway**, 11 km (7 miles) southeast of the centre in San Francisco de Paula (you will have to take a taxi). Though you cannot go inside the graceful bungalow villa, by peering through windows and doors you can

Cars considered collectors' items outside of Cuba are a common sight in Havana.

Hemingway's Finca Vigía — the trophy heads were added after the author's death.

see all the rooms furnished as he had them, covered in bullfighting posters and filled with more than 9,000 books, including such titles as *The Guide to Hunting and Fishing in Cuba*. Excellent photos adorn his office in the adjacent tower, and you can roam the lush gardens searching out his motor boat, the *Pilar*.

Hemingway kept the *Pilar* 10 km (6 miles) to the east of Havana at **Cojímar**, the probable model for the settlement in *The Old Man and the Sea*. Next to a diminutive fort in the little town's old corner is a Hemingway bust, looking out over the bay. The writer frequented La Terraza restaurant (see page 142) nearby, worth visiting for its many photographs of the author in action.

Further east, approximately 18 km (11 miles) from Havana, the **Playas del Este** (Eastern Beaches) are less charming. They are acceptable for a short break from city life, but you are unlikely to want to spend your whole holiday here. The long, sandy beaches are excellent but often wind-buffeted, whilst the communities behind are sparse or bedraggled.

Few tourists make the trip 11 km (7 miles) south of Havana to the rolling meadows of **Parque Lenin**. Limited public transport and scarce funds have resulted in the closure of many of the park's attractions, but at weekends there are vibrant scenes at a small fairground, its Cuban flavour provided by horseback riding and *guarapo* drinks stands.

South of Parque Lenin is **Expocuba**, a kind of Soviet theme park, the theme being post-revolutionary Cuba. Entire buildings are devoted to earnestly showing off achievements in the fields of energy, construction, and biotechnology, while stalls promote parts of the island like a trade fair. There are wonderful **botanical gardens** directly opposite.

Graham and Ernest

Graham Greene's *Our Man in Havana* was first published in 1958. Not only is it an evocative portrait of sleazy 1950s Havana, with scenes set in still-famous establishments such as the Nacional and Sevilla hotels and the Tropicana nightclub; it's also eerily prescient as the hero — the phony British secret service agent, Wormold — invents drawings of Soviet weapons hidden in the Cuban countryside. Nuclear weapons were discovered in Cuba during the Cuban Missile Crisis in 1962.

Greene was a great supporter of the revolution, praising Castro, the war against illiteracy, the lack of racial segregation, and the support of the arts. However, the presence of forced labour camps in the 1960s upset him greatly.

In one sense Ernest Hemingway's Cuban connections are much more readily available, as they've become part of the tourist fabric. He wrote two books based in Cuba: *The Old Man and The Sea* and *Islands in the Stream*.

As a long-standing island resident, he left many real Hemingway locations: the Finca Vigía (see page 43), Cojímar (see page 44), El Floridita (see pages 34 and 140), La Bodeguita del Medio (see page 139), and the Hotel Ambos Mundos (see page 34). However, despite chummy photos with Castro, Hemingway's views on the revolution are elusive; there is simply no reliable evidence to indicate whether he supported or condemned it.

PINAR DEL RÍO PROVINCE

The finger of land pointing west from Havana contains some of Cuba's finest countryside. The lush Guaniguanico mountain range runs alongside the motorway to the provincial capital of Pinar del Río. In the surrounding patchwork of vividly verdant fields, or *vegas*, two-thirds of the country's tobacco is cultivated. In the beautiful Viñales valley, tobacco fields and limestone outcrops combine in spectacular scenery that looks more like Southeast Asia than the Caribbean. Scenes of oxen tilling red-earth fields and cowboy peasants, called *guajíros*, on horseback, are commonplace.

After 63 km (39 miles) on the highway, a turn-off leaves the level, palm-dotted plains for **Soroa**, where a richly endowed botanic garden nestles in the mountain foothills near a tired little tourist complex. A guided tour reveals an orchid garden, exotic fruit trees with lychees and mangoes, coffee plants, and splendid specimens of *jagüey* and *ceiba* trees. A restaurant in the villa of Castillo de las Nubes on a nearby mountain has stunning views.

A proud cake carrier displays his dessert on a sidewalk in Pinar del Río.

At the end of the highway, the small city of **Pinar del Río** is a bustling commercial centre with horse-and-traps laden with local produce trotting in from the surrounding countryside. Along the main street, Calle José Martí, low-rise Neoclassical buildings in blues, yellows, greens, and

Tobacco fields stretch out at the base of one of the many mogotes in the Viñales valley.

oranges, with their pillars in one colour and façades in another, have a stateliness that is undermined by their poor condition. At the eastern end of José Martí, a science museum in an extravagant Gothic/Moorish palace shows fossils and stuffed animals. In backstreet houses, men make homemade cigars, and you'll find an interesting **tobacco factory** housed in an old jail below the Plaza de la Independencia. This and the less picturesque **Casa Garay Rum Factory** on Avenida Isabel Rubio, where they make a local rum liqueur called *guayabita del Pinar*, both welcome visitors.

The road southwest from the city to San Juan y Martinez leads deep into "The Mecca of Tobacco," the **Vuelta Abajo**, where the world's best tobacco is grown. Amid fields of big green leaves ripening in the sun and plantations covered in

Cuban Cigars

The image of a peasant in Communist Cuba with a big fat cigar between his lips seems deeply ironic. Due to an ideal soil and climate, Cuban cigars are the best in the world. Factories produce 350 million a year, with 100 million for export.

There are a number of cigar factories around the island that you can visit. Their rich aroma is overwhelming. Men and women who roll the cigars, called *torcedores*, sit at what look like old-fashioned school desks wrapping poorer-quality leaves in better-quality ones with dexterous ease. While they work, lectors read newspaper and book extracts to them over a microphone. In other rooms, sacks of tobacco leaves are sorted into bundles, cigars undergo quality control tests, and prestigious labels are applied.

Buying a box of cigars can seem daunting. Don't buy one on the street unless you know what you're doing: proper-looking boxes are no assurance of authenticity. In a shop, ask to look inside the box, take out a cigar, see if you like the aroma, and check that it's very slightly springy.

Handmade cigars vary in length from the 4½-inch Demi Tasse to the 9¼-inch Gran Corona. As a rule, bigger cigars are better quality, darker coloured cigars taste sweeter. There are a number of outstanding Cuban brands. Cohibas — dreamt up by Che Guevara and smoked by Castro until he gave up in 1985 — are the world's finest, with a rich and spicy taste. Montecristos are tangy but milder. The H Upmann brand is milder still, while the Romeo y Julieta is famous for its Churchills in individual aluminium tubes. Partagas cigars are strong.

Back home, keep your cigars moist. Either buy a humidor or put the box in a plastic bag with a damp sponge.

canvas sheets for the all-important cigar-wrapper leaves stand gorgeous wooden barns called *casas de tabaco* (tobacco houses). Here, leaves are hung on poles with a needle and thread to turn from green to brown.

Some 27 km (17 miles) to the north of Pinar del Río lies the most picturesque corner of Cuba. The **Viñales valley** is spattered with *mogotes*, sheer-sided limestone masses covered in thick vegetation, the remnants of a plateau which collapsed in the Jurassic period. Tobacco (of lesser quality than

the Vuelta Abajo's) grows in a patchwork of fields below and dries in *casas de tabaco*, here constructed with shaggy thatch. Sun-wrinkled, cigar-chewing *guajíros* in enormous straw hats urge on their oxen, while

> **Full tank, please!**
> *Liénolo, por favor.*
> **(lyaynayloa por fabhor)**

egrets balance on cows' heads, and pink-headed vultures swoop overhead. Come evening, the locals relax in rocking chairs on the verandas of their rustic huts, watching the setting sun turn the sky a deep violet. At any time of day, wander into the fields and meet the farmers, who may smother you with hospitality (cigars, coffee, and so forth) and pose for photos.

The best valley views can be had from the Hotel Los Jazmines (see page 132). The villagey town of **Viñales** is surprisingly spruce, with a fetching arcaded main street and lovely rustic scenes down the back lanes. A couple of local tourist sights have curiosity value. One *mogote* just west of town was painted by workmen dangling on ropes in the 1960s with a **Mural de la Prehistoria** that is 120 metres (370 feet) high and 180 metres (550 feet) long. It depicts evolution from an ammonite to a dinosaur to *homo sapiens*. Just to the north of town, the extensive **Cueva del Indio** was used as a hideout by Indians after the conquest.

A tour through the cave includes an excursion on an underground river in a boat which would-be emigrants once stole for an unsuccessful escape attempt to Florida. Both mural and cave have decent tourist restaurants.

Cayo Largo and the Isle of Youth

The two main islands in the Archipiélago de los Canarreos, south of western Cuba, could not be more different. Cayo Largo is a tourist enclave, where visitors are never more than a

Visitors are dwarfed by only a section of the huge Mural de la Prehistoria.

few yards from pristine white sands. Yet it's an antiseptic place, devoid of Cubans except those who work there. By contrast, the Isle of Youth sees virtually no tourists except those at the Hotel El Colony (see page 132). They come exclusively for the superb diving (see page 87) from a beach a boat ride away on the island's southwestern tip.

Cayo Largo

This 25-km (16-mile) long island, the most easterly of the Archipiélago de los Canarreos, could be your paradise, if all you're looking for is a dazzling beach and clear blue seas. There's not much else of consequence here, other than mangrove, scrub, half a dozen comfortable hotels with a full programme of entertainment and watersports, and an airport which doubles as a disco.

Turtles nest in the sand at one end of the island. At the other, you can go sailing, diving, and deep-sea fishing or take boat trips from a small port to **Cayo Iguana** to meet these harmless reptiles or to **Cayo Rico** for yet more beaches and a seafood restaurant. But the most popular trip of all is to **Playa Sirena**, an incomparable strip of sand a 10-minute boat ride away, where lobster lunches are laid on.

Some package holidaymakers spend the whole of their holiday on Cayo Largo. Those with low boredom thresholds might consider coming just for the day or for overnight trips on half-hour flights from Havana and Varadero.

Isle of Youth (Isla de la Juventud)

Cuba's largest offshore island, some 50 km (31 miles) in diameter, is said to have been the location for Robert Louis Stevenson's *Treasure Island*; pirates buried their booty here in previous centuries. The island received its jaunty name in the 1970s when as many as 22,000 foreign students, mainly from politically sympathetic African countries, studied here in no fewer than 60 schools.

Castro and his followers once slept here: the hospital ward in the Isle of Youth's Model Prison.

Yet the island fails to live up to its colourful past. The number of foreign students has fallen to less than 5,000. Derelict boarding schools dot the monotonous countryside in the north of the is-

Playa Sirena is reached by boat across the turquoise waters which envelop Cayo Largo.

land, which is mostly covered in pine forests and grapefruit orchards. Even more featureless is the island's virtually uninhabited southern half, a vast swampy and forested nature reserve which you can only explore with a guide. However, there are plenty of virgin beaches to be discovered, and in a slightly dingy cave at **Punta del Este** you can examine enigmatic symbols painted centuries ago by Siboney Indians.

For more accessible entertainment, **Nueva Gerona**, the island's little capital, is moderately attractive, with striped awnings along its smart, pillared main street. Just east of town, the **Presidio Modelo** (Model Prison) is fascinating. The dictator Machado built this copy of an American penitentiary in 1931. It consists of vast circular buildings where some 5,000 prisoners used to live in barbaric conditions, two to a windowless and doorless cell overseen by guards in sinister watchtowers. When Castro and 26 of his rebels were sent here after the storming on the Moncada Barracks, they were treated much better and housed in the hospital. Their ward and the cell in which Castro was kept in solitary confinement have been reconstructed, and other rooms recount the prison's history well.

MATANZAS PROVINCE

The province east of Havana is largely flat sugar-cane country and, indeed, in the 19th century it was Cuba's most important cane-producing region. For today's visitors, however, the focus is on the resort of Varadero, with other opportunities for forays into atmospheric, time-warped towns and to the swamplands of the south coast.

Varadero

With dozens of hotels and restaurants, streetside bars, fast-food cafés. and grocery shops, Varadero is like any large resort the world over, which is why it hardly feels like Cuba at all. The resort's profligacy sticks out like a sore thumb in this land of hardship, and more so year by year as millions of dollars are pumped into new hotel complexes.

The 20-km (12-mile) long, virtually uninterrupted white-sand beach with shallow, clean waters is the main attraction, described immodestly by the authorities as the most beautiful in the world. It attracted millionaires in the 1920s, who built palatial holiday villas. Tourism started properly after World War II, with the construction of casinos and such establishments as the Hotel Internacional.

Nowadays, aside from the beach, many people cannot find a good word to

In Cárdenas, the horse-and-trap and bicycle are the most common forms of transport.

say about the resort. It is certainly insulated from real Cuba; there is often a strong smell from the oil pumps on the resort's outskirts; prostitution and hassling is constant and blatant. Moreover, the resort is spread out over 17 km (11 miles), with no real centre, so you need transport to get around. To its credit, however, it has many very comfortable hotels, guaranteed nightlife, and an excellent range of watersports. If you tire of the beach there are organized excursions to every conceivable point of interest on the island, including Havana, only an hour and a half's drive away.

Varadero occupies a long, thin insular spit of sand, with water on both sides and a bridge to the mainland. Colourful pre-revolutionary villas, now part of hotel complexes, make the western extremity of the resort the most attractive. Glass-bottomed boat trips, the most popular excursion, leave from the Hotel Paradiso at the western tip. Between calles 25 and 54 there's something of a local community, with ancient Cadillacs parked outside rickety wooden bungalows. Calles 54 to 64 is the liveliest area, with a shopping mall, a host of restaurants, streetside bars, and the **Retiro Josone**, a pretty park set around a palm-fringed boating lake.

Spreading for several miles farther east are the newest of the hotel complexes and also the restaurant, **Las Américas** (see page 133), an opulent beachside mansion completed by the French millionaire Irenée Du Pont in 1930.

Matanzas and Cardenas

Though just spitting distance from Varadero, these quintessentially Cuban towns are a world apart. Their more-or-less empty shops, dusty backstreets, and primitive transport provide Varadero's package holidaymakers with a convenient insight into everyday Cuban life.

Miles of sand and aquamarine sea explain why Varadero is Cuba's top tourist destination.

Matanzas, 42 km (26 miles) west of Varadero, is busy and grimy. Behind a deep bay, it came into its own during the 19th century when it served as the country's sugar capital. On the classic, leafy main square, Parque Libertad, the **Museo Farmaceutico** is a wonderfully preserved chemist's shop, founded in 1882. It has hundreds of pretty porcelain pots lining its shelves above a long marble serving counter, and medicine cupboards with bottles of ancient remedies made from the likes of eucalyptus and banana extract. Behind the counter you'll find pestles and mortars, old reference books, and antique prescription registers in the dispensary, as well as copper distillation equipment in the laboratory.

The **Hotel Louvre** just next door is a grand, run-down old building with two ferny courtyards — an atmospheric place for a slow drink. On a street running east towards the bay, the **cathe-**

This pharmacy on Matanzas' Bay was founded by Dr. Ernest Triolet in the 1800s.

dral is notable for its many murals, some restored, some badly in need of repair. A little farther to the east, impressive buildings on Plaza de la Vigía include the blue **Palacio de Junco**, which houses a second-rate provincial museum, and the **Teatro Sauto**. Constructed in 1863, the lovely theatre has tiers of wrought-iron boxes and a muralled ceiling; there are performances most weekends.

Las Cuevas de Bellamar, a few kilometres to the south, are Cuba's oldest tourist site; the caves were discovered by chance in 1861 by a Chinese slave. Tours (in English) take you down into a vast chamber to admire the many stalactites and stalagmites.

Fortunes have changed for **Cárdenas**, 15 km (9 miles) to the east of Varadero. Once the island's most important port for sugar exportation, it's now a ramshackle place with long shopping queues and dozens of horses and carts streaming up and down its main street — essential transport here, not a tourist gimmick as it is in Varadero. The main square with its statue of Columbus is an elegant feature, and the **Museo Oscar Maria de Rojas** at Avenida 4 and Calle 12 houses a quirky and varied collection of items, from slaves' manacles to a 19th-century funeral coach and two fleas all dressed up to dance.

Zapata Peninsula

This is the largest wetlands in the Caribbean, flat as a pancake and covered in mangrove swamps and grassland plains. Its protected wildlife includes crocodiles, manatees, and numerous species of birds. Some are endemic to Cuba, such as the tiny bee hummingbird (the smallest bird in the world) and the tocororo, the national bird, while a few are endemic to the swamp, like the Zapata wren and rail. Frankly however, you are unlikely to see any interesting wildlife unless you take a guided bird-watching trip from Playa Larga (see below).

You can see penned reptiles at the crocodile farm at **La Boca**. At this popular tourist site you can also pose with a baby croc and try crocodile steak! A more appealing prospect is picturesque **Guamá**, a half-hour boat ride from La Boca along an artificial channel and then across the vast **Laguna del Tesoro** (Treasure Lake). Legend has it that the lake received its name because the Indians threw their valuable possessions into the water when the Spanish *conquistadores* arrived. Guamá is a group of tiny islands connected by wooden bridges. A few visitors stay in the thatched *cabañas* (see page 134), but most just come to wander along the boardwalk, greeting the ducks and egrets and having a meal. Between May and September beware of the mosquitoes.

South of La Boca you soon come to Bahía de Cochinos, the **Bay of Pigs** (see page 59). At irregular intervals along the often crab-infested road stand concrete memorials to those who died during the invasion of 1961. There are two simple, isolated bungalow hotel complexes on the bay, one at quiet **Playa Larga** (see page 134), the other at **Playa Girón**, where the already scruffy beach is further spoiled

The Guamá boardwalk is peopled with statues of inhabitants of a Taino settlement.

by a concrete breakwater. One major attraction, however, is the excellent Museo Playa Girón, which serves as an emotive memorial to the unsuccessful Bay of Pigs invasion.

CENTRAL CUBA

Tourists usually whiz through central Cuba. The only tourist honeypots are on the coasts, in the south around Cienfuegos' bay and at Trinidad, and in the north at the small resorts of Cayo Coco and Guillermo and Playa Santa Lucía. Elsewhere, those who pause to explore can feel like goldfish in a bowl: as a foreigner, you're a novelty and a source of tremendous interest.

Central Cuba comprises five provinces: from west to east, Cienfuegos, Villa Clara, Sancti Spíritus, Ciego de Avila, and Camagüey. Each focuses on a provincial city of the same or similar name, most of which are of some interest, yet none likely to detain you for longer than a day. The west has the best scenery in the lush Sierra del Escambray mountains. To the east of Sancti Spíritus, towns are unremitting flat plains unfolding to the horizon. Here, sugar cane as high as three men grows in abundance, lorries trundle around with outlandish hairdos of cane, and chimneys of sugar-cane factories poke skywards like towers of cathedrals. In Camagüey, the cattle ranch province, rusty watermills punctuate the sky-line, and *vaqueros* (cowboys) slouch on horses with dangling machetes and lassoes at the ready.

Cienfuegos

The best feature of this important port (250 km/150 miles southeast of Havana) is its position, set at the back of a large bay. Despite industry on its periphery the centre is very attractive, with plenty of colourful neoclassical buildings.

The focal point is **Parque José Martí**, one of the grandest squares in the country. Here you will find the monumental red-domed government offices, an early 19th-century cathedral with a startling gold-painted interior, and a *casa de la trova* (see

---

The Bay of Pigs Invasion

On 17 April 1961, a force of 1,297 Cuban exiles landed at Playa Girón. The Cubans were CIA-trained and came from U.S. ships waiting offshore; U.S.-piloted planes had bombed Cuban airfields days before. For political reasons, however, President Kennedy was unwilling to commit U.S. troops on the ground or order further air strikes. As a result, Castro's 20,000 troops, assisted by artillery and tanks, repelled the invasion within just 48 hours. Some 1,180 exiles were captured and ransomed for $53 million worth of food and medicine. The victory greatly boosted Castro's domestic and international status, and soon after he declared Cuba a socialist, one-party state.

The emotive museum at Playa Girón naturally portrays the events as a great triumph against the United States, and the exiles as rich, corrupt "mercenaries." There are military relics from the battle and plenty of classic war photos, including a famous picture of Castro leaping down from a tank. One wall, devoted to those who died, displays photos and personal possessions.

The fine Teatro Tomás Terry in Cienfuegos, where you may be able to see the ballet.

page 92) with whimsical flourishes.

Take a guided tour of the **Teatro Tomás Terry** on the north side of the square. Built in 1890, it was named after a rich sugar plantation owner. The theatre has a lovely frescoed ceiling and a semicircle of tiered boxes. Enrico Caruso and Sara Bernhardt once performed here, and at weekends you may be able to catch a performance by one of Cuba's top ballet companies.

In the pedestrianized street connecting the square to the Prado, the whole of Cuba's arcane shopping system is on show. The Prado itself is the principal thoroughfare, a tree-lined boulevard full of strollers and lined with classical-style buildings adorned with elaborate balustrades and arcades. The Prado takes you down to the spit of land protruding into the bay past smart waterside villas. Tourists are berthed in the Hotel Jagua (see page 134), next to the fantastical **Palacio del Valle**, a Moorish palace finished in 1917 whose ceilings and walls are covered in patterned stonework.

At the mouth of the bay, on the western side, the **Castillo de Jagua** was constructed by the Spanish to ward off pirates in 1732 (long before the city was founded in 1819). The fort sits next to a pretty fishing community and close to a sign with letters the height of a house that greets arriving tankers with *"Bienvenidos a Cuba Socialista"* (Welcome to

Socialist Cuba). You reach the castle on a tiny ferry from the Hotel Pasacaballo on the eastern side of the bay. Close to the hotel is the best beach in the area, **Playa Rancho Luna**. The **Jardín Botánico,** 18 km (11 miles) outside Cienfuegos, is the oldest botanical garden in Cuba and one of the finest tropical gardens in the world (ask at the tourist office in Cienfuegos about guided tours of the gardens).

Trinidad

The scenic, undulating 72-km (45-mile) road east from Cienfuegos to Trinidad skirts the foothills of the Sierra del Escambray. Forested mountains provide a fitting backdrop to this quietly bewitching town. The third of Diego Velázquez's original seven settlements, it subsequently became rich through the smuggling, slave, and sugar trades. Its sizeable old town is consequently endowed with some marvellous Spanish colonial architecture, and has duly been accorded the title of a UNESCO World Heritage Site.

Carefully restored mansions of the well-to-do have been turned into museums, while art galleries, craft shops, and restaurants occupy more lovely old buildings. In its back-streets, pink, yellow, and rose-coloured façades line cobbled streets whose texture matches the ubiquitous red-tiled roofs. The paving soon gives out as the streets steepen and become rutted tracks which peter out into banana groves. No traffic, not even bicycles, can cope well with Trinidad's street surfaces, so peace reigns. Only crowing cockerels and mobs of angelic, chewing-gum hungry kids break the silence. Locals gently snooze in rocking chairs behind long, wrought-iron grilled windows or inside pretty court-yard gardens flourishing with greenery. In short, the 20th century has hardly encroached on this wonderfully somnolent outpost.

*The scenic Valle de los Ingenios (Valley of the Sugar Mills)
— a source of Trinidad's prosperity in the 19th century.*

The old town centres around the **Plaza Mayor**, a self-con-
sciously pretty square thanks to its railings, fanciful urns,
greyhound statues, and brightly painted colonial buildings.
To one side of the comparatively plain church, the **Museo
Romántico** affords fine views from its balcony and contains
splendid aristocratic furniture. The square's two other little
museums both have attractive courtyards and cool interiors.
The **Museo de Arqueología Guomuhaya** shows bones of
Indians and slaves along with a few stuffed animals, while
the **Museo de Arquitectura Trinitaria** has examples of
woodwork, ironwork, stained glass, and statuary from
around the town.

Rather more interesting is the **Museo Nacional de la Lucha Contra Bandidos** (National Museum of the Struggle against the Bandits), housed in a former convent just to the north of the square. The bandits in question were counter-revolutionary rebels who hid in the Escambray Mountains during the 1960s. On display are *yanqui* ("Yankee," U.S.) weaponry and a captured U.S. reconaissance plane, along with Che's hammock and a roll-call in honour of those who died fighting for socialist Cuba. However, the stupendous 360-degree view from the landmark yellow belfry tower — subject of many a Cuban brochure cover — is the big draw (see page 6).

A block south of Plaza Mayor on Calle Simón Bolivar stands the grand Palacio Cantero, built in 1830. Painted pillars, scrolls, shells, pediments, and drapes embellish the interior, eclipsing the historical artifacts and old furniture assembled inside as the **Museo Histórica Municipal**.

Farther afield, as a focus for your wanderings, head up to the bricked-up church on a hill overlooking the town where boys energetically fly homemade kites, and east down to Plaza Santa Ana (see page 143).

Trinidad's prosperity in the 19th century came from the fruits of 50 sugar mills nearby in the scenic **Valle de los Ingenios**, the Valley of the Sugar Mills, also part of the UNESCO World Heritage Site. Some 13 km (8 miles) to the east of town at Manacas-Iznaga you can look around a lovely colonial hacienda house and its startling rocket-shaped **Torre de Manacas-Iznaga**. From the top of the tower the Iznaga family would keep watch over their slaves toiling in the fields.

Beachaholics should head to **Playa Ancón**, about 12 km (7 miles) from Trinidad, an excellent strip of sand offering a good choice of watersports, a coral reef offshore, and two hotels (see page 135).

Sierra del Escambray

While more compact than the eastern and western ranges on the island, the **Escambray Mountains** (Sierra del Escambray), coated in luxuriant vegetation, are arguably Cuba's most beautiful and are easily accessible. Take the road west of Trinidad for the steep 15-km (9-mile) climb through forests of palms, eucalyptus, and pines to the health resort of **Topes de Collantes**. This purpose-built complex boasts impressive facilities, though it lacks much in the way of life.

A good road (unmarked on some maps) continues north into the mountains past waterfalls and on to **Jibacoa**, the main community in a fertile valley oozing with banana and coffee plantations. Floral gardens envelop colourful clapboarded huts, horses and cattle graze on riverside pastures, and the only traffic comes in the form of open trucks full of *campesinos* (peasants) in sombreros. Life may look idyllic, but it's hard, so the government rewards locals with extra rations.

The plains lying beyond Manicaragua are tobacco country — some of the riches in Cuba. Some 23 km (14 miles) west of Manicaragua you'll come to the artificial **Lago Hanabanilla**, idyllically surrounded by ridged hills dotted with palms. The only eyesore in the area is the large Hotel Hanabanilla (see page 135).

The serene Hanabanilla Lake, backdropped by the Sierra del Escambray.

On a weekend afternoon, the main square of Santa Clara is filled with a cacophony of music.

Santa Clara and Sancti Spíritus

Few tourists make it to these provincial capitals. Come to **Santa Clara** (300 km/180 miles from Havana) on a weekend, when its citizens create a carefree atmosphere in the elegant main square. You might catch a band playing in the bandstand, toddlers trooping round it on goat and cart rides, and Afro-Cuban music simultaneously bellowing from the Baroque *casa de la trova* (see page 92). Also on the square, in a 19th-century mansion, is the **Museo de Artes Decorativas**, whose rooms are graced by a sprightly collection of period Cuban-made furniture as well as attractive French and Chinese porcelain. Near the train station, the **Tren Blindado** (Armoured Train) is historically interesting. Here are small exhibitions inside three wagons from the troop train which Che Guevara derailed in December 1958, days before the revolution triumphed.

Sancti Spíritus, 80 km (49 miles) east, has a fuller history, being another of Velázquez's original townships. However, it's only likely to entertain you for an hour or two. From the town's pleasant main square wander two blocks south to the

Hemingway once patrolled the shores of Cayo Coco for Germans and birds.

Parroquial Mayor, a venerable yellow towered church whose early 16th-century origins make it the country's oldest, and across to the nearby **Museo de Arte Colonial**. This 18th-century mansion has two peaceful courtyards and a succession of grandly furnished rooms, suffused with a gentle light entering through stained-glass windows.

Cayo Coco and Cayo Guillermo

These offshore cays can be reached via a road north of Ciego de Avila, through pineapple orchards and the town of Morón, whose arcaded main street is notable for being virulently pink. Finally, the road becomes a causeway (built in 1987, and still unmarked on most maps) so long (28 km/17 miles) that you can't see land at the far end as you set off.

Cayo Coco doesn't translate as Cay Coconut, as you might expect, but as Cay Ibis, as remarked in Hemingway's *Islands in the Stream*; the author patrolled these shores in World War II looking for Germans. Ibises and other wading birds, sometimes pink flamingoes, can be seen balancing in the brackish waters around the principal causeway and a smaller causeway connecting the cay to **Cayo Guillermo**.

It's the superb sandy beaches and intense blue waters which draw holidaymakers to the area. There's nothing else of interest: both these cays are covered in forest or thick undergrowth, and there are no settlements whatsoever (the only

Cubans who visit are workers). Excursions are usually undertaken on charter flights from an airstrip on Cayo Coco.

Plans are afoot to build hotels all along the 22 km (14 miles) of shell-shaped beaches on Cayo Coco, but presently accommodations are limited. A wide range of non-motorized watersports is available to hotel guests; diving and safaris are popular. Cayo Guillermo's single hotel offers a similar gamut of watersports alongside the shallowest of waters. If you hire a moped or Jeep from either hotel, there are virgin beaches to discover.

Camagüey

The cattle-grazed plains that make up the province of Camagüey hold very little water, so long ago the citizens of Cuba's third-largest city (population 300,000) fashioned enormous earthenware pots to catch and store rainwater. Called *tinajones*, they still adorn many squares and courtyard patios.

*Giant clay jars (*tinajones*), a symbol of Camagüey, can be found all over the city.*

Founded on the north coast in 1514 as Santa María del Puerto Príncipe, the settlement soon moved inland to escape the constant pirate attacks. The town's labyrinthine layout was designed to confuse attackers. Now it disorientates the few tourists who venture into its narrow backstreets.

Camagüey, about 550 km (330 miles) southeast of Ha-

The restrained old façades of Camagüey hide picturesque courtyards within.

vana, lays claim to no special architectural flourishes or must-see sights. Yet its restrained old façades hide picturesque courtyards and there are some half-dozen squares, each boasting a crumbling and (usually) still functioning old church; the city prides itself on its religiousness. On the main shopping street, **Avenida República**, numerous places offer to mend things such as watches, shoes, spectacles, and tyres. Vendors sell inedible-looking cakes, and the only establishments with anything worth buying are dollar shops, invariably tucked away behind closed doors.

Near the train station, the **Museo Casa de Ignacio Agramonte** is named after the city's most famous son, a general from the Ten Years' War (see page 16). It contains stuffed animals from Cuba and around the world, a reasonable art gallery, and examples of old Cuban furniture, but most enjoyable is its courtyard for the *tinajones* beneath exotic fruit trees.

Agramonte was born (1841) at the **Casa Natal de Ignacio Agramonte**, a handsome early 19th-century mansion on Plaza de los Trabajadores, back in the city centre. The patriot is remembered through personal effects; he met his death in battle in 1873 and a copy of his death notice is headed "¡Viva España!" Visit the **La Merced** church opposite to see its peeling frescoes and the venerated objects stored in its crypt.

A dashing equine statue of Agramonte forms the centre-piece of **Parque Agramonte** to the south. The cathedral occupies one side of the park, and the **Casa de la Trova** (see page 92), around a floral patio, puts on musical performances most afternoons. A ten-minute walk west down Calle Cristo brings you to a dignified 18th-century church, behind which spreads a great sea of crosses and marble saints in an interesting cemetery.

Saving Camagüey's best for last: **Plaza San Juan de Dios** is an old cobblestoned square surrounded by brightly hued, single-storey buildings dating from the 18th century (two have picturesque restaurants; see page 143) and a lovely yellow church alongside a restored former hospital.

Playa Santa Lucia

Approximately an hour and a half's drive from Camagüey, at Playa Santa Lucía on the north coast, are resort hotels strung along a fine peninsular strip of sand. Each backs directly onto the beach. A superb coral reef lies offshore and diving here is excellent. Aside from a couple of roadside bars, however, nightlife is limited to hotel entertainment. The only other drawbacks are the mosquitoes, as voracious as anywhere on the island.

A bus service visits **Playa Los Cocos** (Coconut Beach), some 5 km (3 miles) away, a strong contender for the title of Cuba's most beautiful beach, with its aquamarine, sheltered waters. Next door

Playa Los Cocos, a strong contender for Cubas's most beautiful beach.

is a very small community of waterside shacks with fish restaurants, called **La Boca**.

To counter the isolation of Playa Santa Lucía, visitors to the resort are offered a wide range of excursions, including a rodeo at Rancho King, deep-sea fishing, and boat and helicopter trips for days on the beach at unspoiled cays like Cayo Sabinal and Cayo Saetía (see opposite).

ORIENTE

The former, pre-revolutionary province of **Oriente** (meaning "East") is both scenically and historically far more interesting than central Cuba. It incorporates the post-revolutionary provinces of Holguín, Granma, Santiago de Cuba, and Guantánamo. Its many stunning landscapes vary from the north coast's exuberant banana and coconut groves clustered round thatched huts that have changed little from the Indians' *bohíos*, to the towering peaks of the Sierra Maestra mountains, barren and virtually uninhabited on their southern side.

The wars of independence began here during the 1860s, and Castro's power base during the 1950s lay in the Sierra Maestra. There are stirring monuments and museums galore recalling these periods in and around Bayamo and Santiago de Cuba, the latter dubbed Hero City for its many historic patriots.

Holguin Province

The city of **Holguín** (760 km/495 miles southeast of Havana) is busy and not particularly attractive. If you're passing through, look in on the main square for its Art-Deco theatre, art gallery, and eclectic display of historical exhibits inside the **Museo Provincial**. The fine **Carlos de la Torre Natural History Museum**, just south of the square on Calle

Fishermen tend to their boats at the harbourside of pretty little Gibara.

Maceo, in another colonial mansion, has a large collection of indigenous snail shells in dazzling colours.

The province improves considerably as you travel north, where the countryside is lusher. **Guardalavaca**, 60 km (37 miles) from Holguín, is Cuba's prettiest resort, ringed by banana plantations and facing a gorgeous beach backed with a wood of sea-grape trees. Watersports are excellent here and at the equally pretty beach of **Estero Ciego**, 2 km (about a mile) west.

Fuel types for cars/trucks: unleaded (*sin plomo*), regular (*gasolina*), premium (*super*), diesel (*gas-oil*)

The most popular excursion from the resort is by helicopter to **Cayo Saetía**, an island at the entrance of Bahía de Nipe. This is paradise, with unspoiled sands, limpid waters, and Jeep safaris to sight imported wildlife such as antelope and zebra.

If your budget won't stretch to that, there's plenty to explore in Guardalavaca's lovely environs. You can take a boat trip into the middle of Bahía Naranjo to a simple **aquarium** where you can swim with the dolphins. Farther to the west is **Bahía de Bariay**, with a monument confirming that this is the most commonly accepted place for Columbus' landing. Beyond is **Gibara**, a captivating, sleepy little port.

About 6 km (4 miles) south of Guardalavaca amid a verdant forest of lofty palms and thatched homesteads is **Chorro de Maíta**, the Caribbean's most important excavated Indian burial ground. Looking at the 61 skeletons, dating from 1490 to 1540, you can notice how skeletons in pre-conquest graves lie in a foetal position, while post-conquest ones lie in a Christian pose, outstretched with arms folded.

Thick banana groves coat the hillsides along the scenic route south to **Banes**, a tumbledown town of clapboard houses with corrugated roofs. Its **Museo Indo Cubano** has fascinating finds from Chorro de Maíta, such as quarzite necklaces, beakers fashioned from shells, and idols made from mud.

Granma Province

The province takes its name from the yacht which landed near its southwestern tip bearing Castro, Che, and their supporters (see page 19). Roadside rice paddies and cane plantations thousands of acres in size fill its flat northern plains, overseen by the forested northern slopes of the Sierra Maestra.

Bayamo (750 km/490 miles southeast of Havana) is the modest capital. Its fame rests with its contribution to the 19th-century struggle for independence. So many buildings bear a tablet commemorating one hero or another that it could be nicknamed Plaque City. The city's greatest hero is

Carlos Manuel de Céspedes, called nothing less than the Father of the Nation. Near the beginning of the Ten Years' War, on 20 October 1868, his rebel army captured the city from the Spanish. The national anthem, composed by Perucho Figueredo, was sung for the first time in the main church.

The **Casa Natal de Carlos Manuel de Céspedes** (Céspedes' birthplace) was one of the buildings that survived and is now a museum full of his medals and keepsakes, a printing press on which the first free newspaper in Cuba was published, and antiques. The house stands in the seductive, arboreal main square, **Plaza de La Revolución**, where interesting statues of Céspedes and Figueredo face

At Marea del Portillo, bongainvillea-backed beaches attract the solitary wanderers.

one another. On weekend evenings, the square hosts something resembling a large party, with hundreds of Bayamese dressed to the nines, socializing and eating *rosquitas*, the local sweet made of *yuca*.

Next to Céspedes' house is a splendid **Museo Provincial de Granma**, whose best exhibit is a guitar made by a shoemaker with 19,109 pieces of wood. Don't miss the lovely church, next to which the national anthem was sung in the **Plaza del Himno**

Southwest of Bayamo, a road through Bartolomé Masó heads into Cuba's most impressive mountains,

Manzanillo's gazebo has jagged arches, multicoloured tiles, and Arabic lettering.

the **Sierra Maestra**. Some inclines are so steep that a full car may have difficulty. An hour's drive will bring you to the Villa Turistica Santo Domingo (see page 137), from where excursions go up the Pico Turquino, which at 1,982 metres (6,502 feet) is Cuba's highest peak.

Moving back down to the plains: **Manzanillo** is an important industrial port for the exportation of sugar. On clear evenings you can see the sun descend into the sea as a great orange ball. The town is uninspiring apart from some rather outlandish Moorish architecture in the main square: a ri-

74

otous gazebo, wedding-cake fountains and sphinx statues, and a *casa de la cultura* with a tiled courtyard depicting Columbus' landing.

The Céspedes trail continues just southwest of Manzanillo at the remains of his sugar plantation *finca* (country house), **La Demajagua**. Here, on 10 October 1868 (now the occasion for a national holiday), he issued his call for independence, and the bell he rang to free his slaves is enshrined in a wall. Farther southwest at isolated **Playa Las Coloradas**, the clock moves forward to 1956. The mangrove swamp where Castro's boat *Granma* landed has been made a national park, complete with a little arena for rallies.

The only tourists for miles stay in **Marea del Portillo** on the south coast. The dark-brown sandy beach here can't compete aesthetically with dazzling strands elsewhere, but a fine solitary location with daunting, desolate mountains as a backdrop. Horseback trips deep into the *sierra* are popular.

From Marea del Portillo you can travel by chauffeured Jeep along the spectacular coastal road to Santiago. Here, folds of scree-covered mountains plunge into the sea.

Santiago de Cuba

Spend at least a couple of days in Cuba's second city (population 420,000). Enclosed by the Sierra Maestra in a south-facing bowl, **Santiago de Cuba** (880 km/528 miles southeast of Havana) can be enervatingly hot, but at the same time seductively languid. Santiagueros negotiate their hilly streets, keeping to the shady sides, and hang out on delectable overhanging balconies.

Yet Santiago has a singular vibrancy, too. Its predominantly mulatto people, a mix of Spanish, French from Haiti, and huge numbers of African slaves, are persistently friendly. The Afro-Cuban tradition is strong, reflected in its music

Cuba's children — will they preserve Communism or usher in democracy?

(walk down any street and a cacophony of sounds emanates from unseen sources) and particularly in its carnival, now sadly a pale shadow of its former self.

Founded in 1514, Santiago was the island's capital until 1553. Seminal events brought it centre-stage again during the 1950s. The attack on the Moncada Barracks (see page 20), thrust Fidel Castro into the limelight, and it was in the main square on 1 January 1959 that he first declared victory.

Old Santiago

Castro gave his speech from the balcony of the city hall on **Parque Céspedes**. The square lies at the heart of the most atmospheric part of the city, **Old Santiago**, a grid of streets a few blocks inland from the harbour (itself ugly and heavily industrialized). The area is dominated by its twin-towered cathedral. Rebuilt in the 19th century after earthquakes and fires, the cathedral has a handsome interior with carved choir stalls and a frescoed ceiling.

The **Casa de Velázquez,** built in 1516 as the residence of Diego Velázquez, is considered the oldest house in the Americas. The rooms overflow with fine furniture and carved woodwork, and encircle two lovely courtyards.

East from the square, **Calle Heredia** is Santiago's cultural focus. In a few yards you'll come to the **Casa de la Trova** (music society). Most days from mid-morning a succession of groups performs every style of Cuban music. On weekends, the little stage is moved outside, and the whole street may lay on festivities in a "cultural night."

Another place where you can hear Afro-Cuban music at the weekend is the **Museo del Carnaval**, just down Heredia. On Calle Pío Rosado, the **Museo Bacardí** has wide-ranging art, archaeological, and more recent historical collections.

Every street round here is enormously colourful. Two to pick out are **Avenida José A. Saco** (also called Enramada), the main shopping thoroughfare whose faded 1950s signs and ostentatious buildings recall more prosperous times, and cobbled **Calle Bartolomé Masó** (also known as San Basilio). Follow the latter down to the **Padre Pico** steps, which

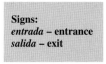

Signs:
entrada – entrance
salida – exit

lead up to the **Museo de la Lucha Clandestina**. This excellent Museum of the Secret Struggle focuses on the activities of the resistance movement against Batista's regime under local martyr Frank País; there are inspiring views from its balcony.

To the west (just south of the train station) is a one-room cigar factory, unimpressive by comparison with other Cuban cigar factories but still an enjoyable place to visit, and the **Ron Caney factory**. This was established in 1838 by Don Facundo Bacardí, but his family fled the country in 1959 and it was nationalized the following year. Tours visit the distillery, the bottling plant, and the giant warehouse where the liquor is left to mature in wooden barrels.

Santiago's Suburbs

A good place to get your bearings on the suburbs of the city is the rooftop bar of the lavish hotel Cubanacán Santiago de Cuba (see page 136), 3 km (2 miles) east of the centre.

☞ In the near distance, you can make out the yellow **Moncada Barracks**, which Castro along with some 135 rebels attacked on 26th of July 1953. The 26 July is now a public holiday, and the barracks have been converted into a school and museum. The museum tells the story of the road to revolution using dozens of memorable photographs. Also on display here are various bloodstained rebel uniforms, some of Fidel's personal effects from his time in the mountains, and "26 Julio" armbands, the name of the resistance movement that developed after the Moncada attack. The bullet holes over the entrance are fake.

☞ The very fine **Cementerio Santa Ifigenia**, just north of the harbour, is stuffed full of Cuban heroes. Pride of place goes to José Martí in a vast octagonal mausoleum, designed so that the tomb catches the sun throughout the day. Also look out for the tombs of Céspedes and Frank País; Frank's (as the *santiagueros* refer to him) is marked like many others with the Cuban flag and the flag of the insurrectional 26 July movement.

Excursions from Santiago

In an impressive setting 7 km (4 miles) from the city is the 17th-century **El Morro Castle** (not to be confused with the castle of the same name in Havana). From its clifftop position, it surveys the harbour mouth. Moated and thickly walled, it houses displays on pirates through the ages.

☞ In just as beautiful a position is the triple-domed church of **El Cobre**, named after nearby copper mines, rising out of the *sierra*'s forested foothills 18 km (11 miles) to the west of Santiago. It contains a statue of a black virgin, the Virgen de la Caridad (Virgin of Charity), the country's patron saint. Pilgrims pray to her image and place offerings of thanks for her miracles.

Package tourists visiting the area stay in hotels to the east of Santiago, spread over the 40-km (25-mile) long **Parque**

Santiago seen from the Museo de la Lucha Clandestina (Musem of the Secret Struggle).

Baconao. The local dark-sand beaches can be scrubby and the hotels themselves are isolated, but there's lots to explore in the park, and the Sierra de La Gran Piedra rises majestically above the coast.

A tortuous side road 12 km (7 miles) east along the coast ascends the mountains to **La Gran Piedra** (The Big Stone), where you can climb on foot for a bird's-eye view of eastern Cuba. About 2 km (about a mile) beyond, a driveable dirt track leads to **Museo La Isabelica**, a 19th-century coffee plantation *finca* (country house) with a workshop, original furniture, and a concrete garden where coffee beans were laid out to dry.

The coastal road continues to **Museo Histórico Granjita Siboney**, the farm from where Castro's rebels left to attack the Moncada Barracks. Photographs and newspaper cuttings tell the story surrounding the events in prosaic fashion.

Another 10 km (6 miles) east is the **Valle de la Prehistoria**, which wins the prize for the country's most bizarre attraction. Goats graze around some 250 massive lifesize statues of dinosaurs and a giant, club-wielding Stone-Age man. A little farther on, the **Museo Nacional del Transporte** is almost as peculiar. Its collection of vintage American cars is being assembled by offering Cubans new Ladas for their old Cadillacs. The park's most picturesque spot is farther to the east at **Laguna Baconao**, where the mountains slumber behind a beautiful, lake. Boat trips are possible, from a horrible little zoo.

Guantánamo Province

You can reach remote and mountainous far-eastern Cuba by continuing along the coast road from Parque Baconao on a memorable, good dirt track and paved road; otherwise you

---

Gitmo Bay

Guantánamo Bay Naval Base has had its share of publicity. First there was a 1992 film starring Tom Cruise and Jack Nicholson, *A Few Good Men*. Then, in 1994, the United States billeted some 15,000 Cuban refugees here, rather than let them stay in the United States.

The base, straddling 117sq km (45 sq miles) across both sides of the bay, is one of the world's strangest political set-ups. The Platt Amendment of 1901 gave control of Guantánamo Bay to the U.S. navy for a peppercorn annual rent of $2,000 (increased to $4,085 in 1934). Castro refuses to cash the cheques. Since the breakdown of American–Cuban relations, both countries have encircled the base in minefields, and the only people who can cross the frontier are a handful of Cubans who have worked on the base since before the revolution.

The base is entirely self-sufficient, down to its own desalination plant for fresh water. A guide from the Hotel Guantánamo (see page 138) takes tourists to a hill overlooking the bay, where he points out Gitmo's features on a plan in a quasi–operations room. Then, from a camouflaged lookout, aided by Russian binoculars, you can pick out the Stars and Stripes, the airstrips, the town of some 7,000 personnel, and the refugees' tent city.

Experienced cigar bundlers in Santiago's one-room cigar factory have refined their occupation into a science.

can backtrack to Santiago. The province only has one conventional tourist destination, the magical little town of Baracoa. The only reason to stop over in the unappealing city of Guantánamo would be to visit the lookout at the American naval base.

The dry, cacti-strewn landscape of the south coast starts to change as you follow the extraordinarily windy, oddly-named La Farola (The Beacon) across the mountains to **Baracoa**. Green hillsides covered with cocoa and coconut groves (local industry revolves around a chocolate and coconut factory) envelop the seaside town, and all around are palm-backed beaches and delightful, sinewy rivers.

That Baracoa was the first settlement to be established by Diego Velázquez in 1511 is not in doubt. However, the locals also claim that Columbus first landed at this spot (not near Gibara, as most historians believe). They insist that he planted the **Cruz de la Parra** (Cross of the Vine), on show in the church on the main square, in the soil on his arrival. Whatever the truth of the matter, carbon dating has established that the cross is more than 500 years old.

In any case, Baracoa doesn't need the appeal of Columbus associations. A good place to get your bearings is the hilltop Hotel El Castillo (see page 138), which looks out over old red-tiled roofs, the town's oyster-shaped bay, and the landmark mountain known as El Yunque (The Anvil), so named on account of its singular shape. The streets below are dreamy in character.

On Calle Antonio Maceo, you'll find people queuing for hot chocolate drinks in the baking tropical sun at the **Casa del Chocolate**. Opposite is a lovely *casa de la trova* (music society), holding rooftop performances. A little farther along, the main square has a striking bust of Hatuey, the brave Indian leader who held out against the early *conquistadores* until he was caught by the Spanish and burned at the stake. Also wander along the **Malecón**, the seaside avenue, from the snug **Matachín Fort** (with a little museum) to the Hotel La Rusa, named after a glamorous Russian emigrée who over the years hosted celebrities from Che and Fidel to Errol Flynn.

The living and the extinct — goats and dinosaurs together in the Valle de la Prehistoria.

Lastly, don't miss the opportunity to come here in the week of 1 April, when heady street parties every night commemorate the disembarkation of General Antonio Maceo at nearby Playa Duaba in 1895, marking the beginning of the War of Independence.

WHAT TO DO

SHOPPING

There is little worth buying in Cuba beyond the obvious souvenirs such as T-shirts, bottles of rum, and cigars. Yet browsing is absolutely fascinating and provides profound insights into Cuba's ravaged and arcane economy.

Hotel shops provide basic such essentials as mineral water, soap, and toothpaste, but many medicinal or cosmetic staples are hard to come by and, when available, can be very expensive; bring all you need from home.

The Cuban Main Street

Chances are you won't find anything you want to buy on any Cuban main street. The majority of shops are barren, colourless places and they accept only pesos. Many items, such as most clothes and food, can only be purchased with a ration book. Shops selling nonrationed goods are generally full of undesirable junk.

Two recent developments, however, have radically altered the face of the Cuban main street. Firstly, in 1993 Cubans were legally allowed to spend dollars, and conse-

A stall at Trinidad's craft market shows an increase in available Cuban souvenirs.

quently dollar shops opened up all over the country. Nowadays queues (lines) form outside signless shopfronts in even
the smallest rural towns as locals wait to buy new clothes,
foreign cigarettes, and foodstuffs like chocolate and cooking
oil. Secondly, in 1994 farmers were given permission to sell
food directly to customers. Each town now has a *mercado
agropecuario* (private market) where meat and groceries are
sold at astronomical peso prices.

Souvenirs to Buy

The biggest bargain is a box of cigars (see page 48), which
cost approximately four times less than back home. Bottles
of rum (see page 97) also offer big savings. When buying
cigars and rum, bear in mind the customs limits (see page
111).

Compact disks and cassettes of Cuban music are widely
available, though choice is limited: be sure to snap up any
recordings you can find of
the excellent contemporary
bands mentioned on page 89.
Musical instruments, such as
maracas and claves, make
good, inexpensive presents.
Local arts and crafts vary
from tacky figurines to
pleasant drawings of street
scenes and post-modernist
portraits. More universally
appealing are the evocative
posters and black-and-white
photos of Fidel, Che, and
company, whose faces ap-
pear also on many a T-shirt.

*Cigar factories that are open
to tourists often have their
own well-stocked shop.*

If you want to read about Cuba's economy and politics from its own viewpoint, there are numerous books, many translated into English.

Where to Shop

Hotel shops sell T-shirts, rum, and often cigars. Better hotels have fashion boutiques, too. Often craft stalls are set up around the pool. ARTEX shops, found the length and breadth of Cuba, sell cultural paraphernalia such as cassettes and books. Cigar factories open to tourists have an affiliated shop selling cigars. Some towns have craft markets, and you may enjoy giving your dollars directly to local people. For airport shopping, see page 106.

There are more interesting things to buy in Old Havana than in the rest of Cuba put together. On most days a lively craft market, with provocative art and lovely hats made from stripped palm leaves, may be found strung across Plaza de la Catedral, while Plaza de Armas is busy with second-hand book vendors. Intriguing, hole-in-the-wall arts and crafts shops are concentrated along Calle Obispo. The excellent Palacio de la Artesanía (at calles Cuba and Tacón) is a souvenir supermarket in a fine old mansion. Prices are high, but the range of T-shirts, cigars, music, and crafts (look for homemade toy Cadillacs) cannot be bettered in Cuba. Bazar La Travesia (on O'Reilly opposite El Floridita) sells a vast range of necklaces, masks and images of gods related to Santería cults (see page 35). Above El Floridita, La Casa del Ron has the island's most impressive selection of rums, from hundred-dollar vintages to half a dozen national brands to rum flavoured with grenadine, peppermint, or banana.

> You're welcome! –
> *De nada.*
> **(day nahdah)**

Trinidad has the best array of crafts shops in the country. Tasteful drawings of the town and assorted prints by Cuban artists such as Wilfredo Lam make splendid gifts. There's also a vibrant daily crafts market on Colón, southwest of Antonio Maceo.

SPORTS

Most resort hotels have tennis courts, a volleyball court, and aerobics sessions. For a nation which uses equine power for much of its transport, it's not surprising that horseback riding is possible at most resorts. Varadero's golf course at Club de Golf Las Américas has recently been expanded to 18 holes.

Watersports

Watersports enthusiasts are especially well served in Cuba. Virtually every resort offers windsurfing, catamarans, canoes, jet skis, and waterskiing. As anywhere in the world, motorized sports are expensive. Watersports centres are almost always affiliated to a particular hotel, but anyone can use the equipment for hire.

Cuba claims to be surrounded by one of the world's largest coral reefs, and more than 1,000 sunken wrecks. There are so many tropical fish—angel-fish, groupers, parrot-fish, moray eels—and sponges that it can feel like swimming in an aquarium.

Diving is the number-one watersport. Facilities are generally excellent, and prices are the lowest in the Caribbean. Nearly every resort has at least one professional diving centre equipped with all the requisite equipment, from oxygen tanks to wetsuits. Most centres offer week-long diving courses for an internationally recognized qualification (such as CMAS or PADI), as well as two-day introductory courses.

Cuba caters for all levels of diving expertise. Here, beginners are put through their paces.

Dozens of diving sites can be reached from resorts, typically a half-hour boat journey away. The diving centre at El Colony Hotel on the Isle of Youth (see page 132) offers the best facilities and diving, but it isn't well suited to beginners. There are 54 designated sites, including caves, wrecks, and what is claimed to be the tallest coral column in the world. Resorts catering for all levels of ability include Cayo Largo, Varadero, Playa Girón (with good diving directly off the shore), Playa Ancón, Cayo Coco, Guardalavaca, and Playa Santa Lucía.

One old man's struggle with a bloody-minded marlin and voracious sharks in Hemingway's *The Old Man and the Sea* has immortalized Cuba's deep-sea fishing. Trips leave from the island's resorts and Havana's Hemingway Marina in search of the likes of marlin, wahoo, and swordfish. In addition, there are offshore expeditions for smaller fry such as tarpon, sea bass, and mackerel. For freshwater fishing, Hanabanilla and Zaza (near Sancti Spíritus) lakes both hold

Cuba's beaches offer diversion for water babies and landlubbers alike.

impressively big, copious large-mouth bass.

Spectator Sports

Cuba regards sporting prowess as very important for its international status. It invests large sums of money in training its sports people, particularly boxers and track-and-field athletes. In 1991, it won more medals than even the United States in the Pan-American Games. You can see an example of this intensive training for yourself at the Gymnastics Academy in Havana (see page 36).

The national sport is baseball. Cuban teams are among the best in the world, probably second only to the U.S. teams. While children improvise with a stick and a makeshift ball in every town's open spaces, the main cities have vast stadia. It can be difficult to find out exactly when a game is taking place—simply ask around. Spectators are extraordinarily passionate, as are the fanatics who gather in Havana's Parque Central to rant about the latest matches and scores.

ENTERTAINMENT

Although cultural activity has been under state control since the revolution, and Havana is no longer sizzling with the infamous Mafia-funded clubs of the 1950s, both high culture and more down-to-earth nightlife are thriving in Cuba. The only problem is that outside the resorts it can be hard to pin down what's going on where. In the resorts, nightlife is focused around hotels, ranging from decent live

bands, dance, and fashion shows to ghastly mimed Beatles'
sing-a-longs.

Cabaret

Even if you find the prospect of cavorting dancers covered in
little more than a G-string and a pair of carefully positioned

---

A Musical Melting Pot

Salsa, rumba, mambo, cha-cha-cha—Cuba's rhythms are
known the world over. Reflecting the mixed heritage of its
people, Cuban music came about towards the end of the
1800s through "the love affair of the African drum and the
Spanish guitar." In a typical Cuban band today you'll hear
Latin stringed instruments in harmony with African bongos,
congas and *batás* (all drums), *claves* (wooden sticks), and
instruments made from hollow gourds such as the maracas
and *güiro*.

First came the style *son,* which permeates all Cuban
music and is the direct forebear of salsa. Mixed with jazz
influences, it led to the brass-band sounds of groups such
as Los Van Van, Isaac Delgado, and Irakere. Cha-cha-
cha arrived in the 1950s, having developed from upbeat
mambo, which in turn was a blend of jazz and the
sedate, European *danzón* of the ballroom. The African
rumba is typified by more erotic dancing—celebratory,
with religious overtones. *Trovas*, or ballads, were sung in
colonial times by troubadors in *casas de la trova* (see
page 92). Since the revolution, the *trova* has adapted
into the *nueva trova*, as sung by Silvio Rodríguez and
Pablo Milanés.

Confused? Rest assured that there's one song you'll soon
be humming and that's Guantanamera. It's cast as the unof-
ficial Cuban anthem, with verses written by the patriot José
Martí.

---

stars off-putting, see a big song and dance show in the flesh (so to speak) before making your final appraisal. Kitsch it might be, smutty it is not. Alongside the vaunted bottom-wiggling you'll find dazzling costumes shimmering in impressive choreographed dance routines, rousing singing with big band orchestras, and even acrobatics. And it's not all just tourist fodder: in many provincial towns, the local hotel lays on a mini–poolside cabaret on weekend evenings.

The Tropicana in Havana, in a dazzling open-air arena, is indisputably the cabaret to end all cabarets. Founded in 1939, the likes of Nat King Cole performed here in pre-revolutionary times. Now the sheer scale of the spectacle, with a 32-piece orchestra and a cast of over 200 (some parading in impossibly large headdresses) assaults the senses. The show regularly kicks off at 9:30 P.M., and at certain times of the year a second, shorter performance follows later. There is also a restaurant and disco. Reservations and transportation can be made at your hotel (you can always visit independently, but the venue, situated in the Marianao suburb at calles 72 and 43, is tricky to find). Havana's next best, but much smaller, cabaret show is at the Hotel Nacional (see page 131), nightly at 10:30 P.M. and 12:15 A.M.

The Tropicana in Santiago de Cuba, in an enormous, recently constructed complex on the city's northern outskirts (signposted from Plaza de la Revolución), is hardly less impressive than Havana's, but is less slick and less gaudy. Of the two nightly shows (from 10:00 P.M.), the former is more romantic, the latter livelier.

In the resort of Varadero, the Cabaret Continental at the Hotel Internacional (see page 133, shows every night from 8:30 P.M. to 3:00 A.M.) pales in comparison with the former venues, but is nonetheless an enjoyable and sometimes fairly raunchy song-and-dance extravaganza. A fun show with a pi-

Calendar of Events

Reliable information on events is hard to come by. Contact the tourist board or a specialist travel agent before making plans.

January: *Carnaval, Varadero.* Lasts the whole month, with nightly street parties and processions once a week. Hotels lay on Cuban dance lessons and competitions.

February: *International Jazz Festival, Havana.* A biennial, week-long coming together of top jazz artists from Cuba and around the world, with workshops, lectures, open rehearsals, and performances.

May: *Hemingway Marlin Fishing Tournament, Hemingway Marina, Havana.* Four-day-long competition begun in 1950 and won by Castro in 1960.

July: *Carnaval, Santiago de Cuba.* Cancelled between 1990 and 1993 because of economic restraints, Cuba's most famous celebrations are gradually being revived, with *comparsas* (street dances) such as congas in various of Santiago's *barrios* (districts) and down Avenida Garzón. A week-long event, focused around 26 July, traditionally to tie in with the end of the *zafra*, or sugar-cane harvest.

November: *Havana International Ballet Festival.* A congregation of top ballet companies from around the world, begun in 1960 and held alternate years.

December: *New Latin American Film Festival, Havana.* The most important film festival in the Spanish-speaking world.

rate theme takes place in a cave at the Cueva del Pirata, some 9 km (6 miles) to the east of Varadero, nightly at 10:30 P.M.

Other Live Music

You certainly won't have to go far out of your way to hear live music. Roving groups of musicians play in every conceivable venue around the country, from airports to restaurants, and just wandering the streets of Havana of an evening you are likely to come across some heady backstreet party with a live band.

Good music can be heard in every town at the *casa de la trova*, usually a fine old building on or near the main square. Performances are both amateur and professional, free and irregular—all of which makes for a wonderful atmosphere—but often take place during the day for the benefit of tourists and on weekend evenings for locals. The most famous casa de la trova is in Santiago (see page 75), while those in towns like Baracoa and Camagüey are especially charming.

One of the more restrained moments from the show at Cabaret Continental.

Probably the best place for live jazz and salsa in the country is the slightly dated Hotel Riviera (Paseo and Malecón, Vedado, Havana). Here, from midnight (except Wednesday), Cuba's very best salsa bands perform in the earthy Palacio de la Salsa (dancing is very much in order), and jazz artists entertain drinkers in the adjacent bar, Thursday to Sunday from 9:00 P.M.

Discos

Maracas, drums, guitar, bass —the classic fusion of European and African sounds.

Discos pulsate to both Latin and western rhythms. The discos in Havana's Hotel Meliá Cohiba (see page 131) and Santiago's eponymous hotel (see page 137) are glitzy affairs; also try El Galeón, in a make-believe pirate ship that sets sail from under Havana's La Cabaña fortress. The best in Varadero is La Bamba at the Hotel Tuxpan. In Guardalavaca, head for open-air La Roca, set just above the beach.

Local Cuban discos, where you'll find some phenomenal dancing, lethal supplies of rum, and a heady atmosphere, can be found on many a town's main square: locals crowd the door but foreigners will usually be ushered in.

Fashion Shows

The country's fashion house is called La Maison, located in Havana at Avenida 7 and Calle 16, Miramar, and in Santiago at Avenida Manduley and Calle 1, Vista Alegre. The shows take place each evening at 9:30 P.M. in leafy courtyards behind grandiose villas full of boutiques displaying the models' clothes.

The Classical Repertoire

Drama, opera, classical recitals, and, above all, ballet can be enjoyed in theatres all around Cuba. Opulent, old-fashioned theatres such as those in Cienfuegos, Camagüey, and Matanzas, not to mention Havana's magnificent Gran Teatro, are sights in their own right. The best way of finding out what's on is to visit the theatre: performances are in many cases limited to weekends.

The Gran Teatro in Havana at calles Prado and San Rafael has a number of concert halls and lays on a wide repertoire of entertainment, from opera recitals to ballet. It is home to the internationally-renowned Ballet Nacional de Cuba; if you hear that the company (or the rather more innovative Ballet de Camagüey) is performing, be sure to snap up tickets.

CHILDREN

At resorts, waterbabies will be happy and those aged around 10 and upwards will be able to join in many of the activities. A few resort hotels, such as at Cayo Coco, have a children's club, and top hotels can organize babysitting. Outside of the resorts, however, only the most inquisitive and broad-minded kids would happily endure the rigours of travel, even though Cubans make a fuss of them.

In some provincial towns at the weekend, toddlers can take rides in goat-pulled carts.

EATING OUT

It is something of a paradox that a land as fertile as Cuba should have such a problem feeding its people, yet during the Special Period, food shortages have become serious. However, those with plenty of dollars (i.e., tourists) are immune from hardships.

Nevertheless, do not come to Cuba expecting memorable gastronomic experiences. Although the fusion of Spanish and African culinary traditions in its Criollo (Creole) cuisine sounds interesting, the results are generally dull (ask if there is a house speciality, usually the most interesting dish available). Many hotels play safe, offering international fare.

Where to Eat

If you're based in a resort, you may end up eating almost all your meals at the hotel. Large hotels often have not only a main buffet restaurant, but also a poolside *parrillada* (grill) and a beachside café.

Restaurants broadly divide into two categories: those for tourists, where the food is usually edible and you must pay in dollars, and those for Cubans, where food is limited and of poor quality, waits are long, and pesos are acceptable. Since

No shortage for tourists: a hotel's buffet spread is a virtual cornucopia.

locals are now able to spend dollars legally, this division has become more lax: Cubans eat at some less expensive dollar restaurants, and some establishments take both dollars and pesos.

In resort hotels and around Havana, cafés serve sandwiches (almost always ham and/or cheese), but otherwise a snack in Cuba is hard to find. Picnic food is an even more difficult proposition: hotel shops sell packs of biscuits and crisps; private farmers' markets sell fruit for pesos.

It is common to be invited to eat in private homes (*casas particulares* or *paladares*—literally "palates") for payment in dollars. For a while they operated clandestinely outside the law, but in 1995 the government legalized them. The food is usually better than in most restaurants and costs considerably less. Establish the price for the whole meal before you sit down. Your hosts will not eat with you, but there *may* be a family atmosphere as you enjoy steak or lobster in the front room of a tenement flat.

Enjoy you meal! –
¡Buen provecho!
(bwayn provaycho)

What to Eat

Breakfast can be the best meal of the day, as many hotels offer buffet spreads with fresh fruit, fruit juices, cheeses, meats, and pancakes. Often there are also eggs, made to order. In more modest hotels, sandwiches and omelettes are generally the staple fare.

Bowls of salads, piles of bananas, chunks of watermelon, cakes galore, a choice of fish, meat, and pasta: those of a sensitive disposition may find the prodigality of the top hotels' buffets disturbing when locals have so little to eat. Those with large appetites will find buffets very good value. The food is "international" rather than typically Cuban.

A fish restaurant in Playa Santa Lucía is located on the very water from which dinner has just been caught.

Most restaurants serve a Creole Cuban cuisine. Its main component is rice and beans, either *moros y cristianos* (literally "moors and christians," or rice and black beans) or *congrí* (rice and kidney beans), typically found in the east of Cuba. Accompanying meat is often pollo asado (roast chicken) or *cerdo asado* (roast pork).

White fish is commonly presented under the generic label *pescado* and is typically fresh and simply grilled; numerous restaurants serve lobster—at a price. Popular side dishes include root vegetables such as *malanga* and *yuca* (cassava), and *maduros* or *tostones* (fried plantains). You may not enjoy the dessert *pasta de guayaba con queso* (cheese in a guava paste), but are sure to love the delicious Coppelia ice-cream, made all over the country.

Drinks

The national drink is *ron*, or rum, produced from cane juice and molasses, the leftovers from the manufacture of sugar. Unaged rum, called *aguardiente* (burning water), is particularly alcoholic. Five- and seven-year-old rum, darkened and flavoured in oak barrels, should be drunk straight or on the rocks.

Cuban cocktails make use of one- or three-year-old white rum. A number have achieved folkloric status: Hemingway drank his mojitos (sugar, lime juice, ice, fresh mint, rum, and soda water) in La Bodeguita del Medio (see page 139) and his daiquiris (sugar, lime juice, and rum blended into crushed ice) in El Floridita (see page 140). Less exotic is the Cuba libre—simply rum and coke, often served with a slice of lime.

> *¡A su salud!* – to your health!

National brands of **beer** include Hatuey, Cristal, Mayabe and Bucanero, all very drinkable, Hatuey particularly so. Only the more expensive restaurants serve **wine**, and the selection is usually limited to a few imported bottles.

Many of Cuba's rum-based cocktails have achieved folkloric status.

As for soft drinks, try wonderfully sweet *guarapo*, pure sugar-cane juice pressed right before your eyes, and a *granizado*, a flavoured water-ice in a paper cone from ubiquitous streetside carts.

Coffee comes with a flourish in Cuba. Ask for either a *café cubano*, served espresso style and traditionally drunk with unimaginable quantities of sugar, or *café américano*, which is weaker and served in a large cup.

To Help You Order...

Could we have a table?	**¿Puede darnos una mesa?**
May I see the menu, please?	**¿Puedo ver la carta, por favor?**
What do you recommend?	**¿Qué me aconseja?**
	I'd like... Quisiera...
I'm a vegetarian.	**Soy vegetariano.**

beer	**cerveza**	milk	**leche**
bread	**pan mineral**	water	**agua mineral**
butter	**mantequilla**	salad	**ensalada**
cocktail	**coctel**	sandwich	**bocadillo/**
coffee	**café**		**bocadito**
dessert	**postre**	seafood	**mariscos**
fish	**pescado**	soft drink	**refresco**
fruit	**fruta**	sugar	**azúcar**
ice	**hielo**	tea	**té**
ice-cream	**helado**	vegetables	**vegetales/**
meat	**carne**		**legumbres**
menu	**carta/menú**	wine	**vino**

And Read The Menu...

arroz blanco	white rice	**langosta**	lobster
asado	roast/grilled	**naranja**	orange
bistec	steak	**papas**	potatoes
camarones	shrimps/prawns	**papas fritas**	chips
cerdo/puerco	pork	**pan tostado**	toast
congrí	rice and beans	**picadillo**	minced meat
frijoles	beans	**plátano banana/**	
frito	fried		plantain
huevos	eggs	**pollo**	chicken
jamón	ham	**queso**	cheese
jugo de fruta	fruit juice	**revoltillo**	omelette

INDEX

Where more than one page reference is given, the one in **bold** refers to the main entry. Page numbers in *italic* refer to an illustration.

101

HANDY TRAVEL TIPS

An A–Z Summary of Practical Information

A number of useful words and phrases have been translated into Spanish, usually appearing in the singular.

A

ACCOMMODATION *(hotel; alojamiento)* (See also CAMPING on page 107, TRAVELLING TO CUBA on page 126, and RECOMMENDED HOTELS on page 130)

Standards and facilities have improved dramatically over the past few years, thanks to heavy investment from and management by Canadian, Spanish, and German companies. Cuba's new or restored hotels in resorts and in Havana typically boast a sculpted swimming pool, a choice of restaurants, impressive buffets, boutiques, and bedrooms with state-of-the-art air-conditioning and satellite TV. Resort hotels offer round-the-clock entertainment, from aerobics and Spanish classes to water-polo matches and best-tan contests. Simpler resort hotels offer some in-house entertainment, and invariably have a pool.

Elsewhere, hotels are much less enticing. Foreigners are billeted in large, Soviet-style concrete eyesores located on the outskirts of towns. While most have plenty of facilities, the pool is often murky and hot water intermittent. Yet rooms are always en suite, and may have a fridge and old-fashioned radio, if not a TV. More characterful but more basic hotels in the centre of towns seldom admit foreigners. Wherever you stay, you may want to bring a rubber stopper for sinks and tubs, as many rooms are not equipped with them.

You're under no obligation to make advance reservations. However, hotels in resorts, Havana, and Santiago de Cuba can be full, particularly around Christmas, New Year, and Easter and in summer. As it can be difficult getting through to phone numbers in Cuba, for reservations from abroad you'd be wise to use a specialist agency in your own country. For reservations in Cuba from one hotel to the next, the receptionist may telephone for you in Spanish (you'll be charged for the call). You can also make reservations in the airport (see below).

Cuba

In **Varadero,** the newest, most expensive hotels are at the far eastern end, a few miles from the centre where the more modest hotels are clustered. In **Havana**, stay in or near Old Havana rather than the business district of Vedado. In **Santiago de Cuba**, you'll probably be staying in the city's suburbs, a short taxi ride from the centre.

I'd like a room...	**Quisiera una habitación**...
with twin beds/with a	**con dos camas/con cama**
double bed	**matrimonial**
What's the price...?	**¿Cuál es el precio?**

AIRPORTS *(aeropuerto)* (SEE TRANSPORT on page 124 and TRAVELLING TO CUBA on page 126)

Cuba's main airport is **Havana's** José Martí, 20 km (12 miles) south of downtown Havana. Terminal 1 has international Cubana and Iberia flights and most domestic flights, Terminal 2 has all other international flights, and Terminal Caribbean some Cayo Largo flights. Hotel reservations can be made at the airport's Infotur office (see TOURIST INFORMATION on page 123) on arrival. Varadero's airport is 22 km (14 miles) west of Varadero. Santiago de Cuba's airport is located 6 km (4 miles) south of the city.

On arrival, if you're on a package holiday, a bus will transfer you to your hotel. Independent travellers can book transfers through specialist agencies in their own country; otherwise take a taxi. On departure, larger airports such as Havana's and Varadero's have a selection of spirits, cigars, and souvenirs for last-minute shopping. At all airports, you have to pay a modest departure tax in dollars.

B

BICYCLE AND MOPED HIRE *(bicicleta; motorino)*

With the scarcity of transport, millions of Cubans now ride bicycles. For tourists, cycling is a good way to get around Havana: contact **Panaciclos**, tel. (07) 810153, (07) 814142. Most resorts have bikes to rent; some tourists bring bikes with them on the plane. Lock your bike to something whenever you're not on it. One with sturdy tyres to cope with the uneven surfaces is best — bring your own spares.

You can rent mopeds in most resorts. No licence is required.

C

CAMPING *(camping)*

Presently, there are only two campsites geared to foreigners. Both have huts *(cabañas)* rather than tents. **Aguas Claras** is 7 km (4 miles) from Pinar del Río on the road to Viñales. **El Abra** is on the coast at Jibacoa, 40 km (25 miles) west of Matanzas. Both are friendly, inexpensive, and attractive, and have a pool, bar, and restaurant. Telephone the organization for camping, **Cubamar**, (07) 300662.

CAR HIRE *(alquiler de automóviles/carros)*
(See also DRIVING on page 111)

There are good reasons for not renting a car in Cuba. It's expensive, as is petrol (gasoline), and rental companies are inefficient and will milk you for every dollar you possess. However, as public transport is so poor, having a car is the only way to explore with any freedom.

To rent a car, you must be at least 21 years old and have had a year's driving experience. You will need to present your national or an international driving licence.

Reservations. The three main car-rental companies are Havanautos, Transautos, and Nacional, with dozens of offices and rental centres throughout the island. You can book a car through some specialist companies in your home country, at a local office or through their central reservations offices (Havanautos (07) 332369/332891, Transautos (07) 335532/406217/409200/ 413906), and Nacional (07) 810357.

Costs and insurance. Companies offer virtually identical rates. With limited mileage rates you pay an exorbitant 30 cents for every kilometre over 100 km per day, so opt for the unlimited mileage rates.

Insurance must be paid locally even if you have pre-paid the car rental abroad. If there is any damage to the car, you must pay the first few hundred dollars' worth of repair unless you can prove the accident wasn't your fault. You must leave a cash or open credit card guarantee to cover for this eventuality. Inspect the car thoroughly before you set off to identify existing dents and scratches.

Cars. While the locals drive around in 1950s Cadillacs or 1980s Ladas, tourists are treated to fairly new cars such as Peugeots and Renaults. Less expensive models are not equipped with air-conditioning. Renting a Jeep has drawbacks and advantages: while it guzzles petrol and may be a soft-top, exposing passengers to the burning sun and luggage to prying fingers, the rigours of potholes and untarmacked roads become inconsequential.

Drop offs. For a fee, you can pick up a car from one car rental office and leave it in another. For example, you could rent a car in Havana, drop it off in Santiago, and fly back to Havana.

Petrol. You must pay for whatever petrol (gasoline) there is in the car when you pick it up. You can claim back any petrol left over when you return the car. Make sure you're provided with a list of Cupet fuel stations (see DRIVING, page 111). Lastly, rent a car whose fuel cap is lockable: syphoning fuel is not uncommon.

Make sure you've been given phone numbers to ring should you break down. Check the car's spare tyre is pumped up and that there is a jack: Cuba's potholed roads mean punctures are commonplace. Rental cars are very conspicuous. Hide away all items at all times.

I'd like to rent a car.	**Quisiera alquilar un automóvil/carro.**
for a day/a week	**para un día/una semana**

CLIMATE and CLOTHING

The chart below shows the *average daily temperature* in Havana. For beach lovers and sightseers, March to May is the ideal time to visit. December and January can at times be too overcast for the beach. The more active should avoid the height of summer when it's debilitatingly hot. The summer months are also the wettest and hold a small risk of hurricanes. As for regional variations, the mountains are cooler, and the south and east drier and a little warmer.

	J	F	M	A	M	J	J	A	S	O	N	D
°F	79	79	81	84	86	88	89	89	88	85	81	79
°C	26	26	27	29	30	31	32	32	31	29	27	26

Clothing. During the day, you'll rarely need more than a swimming costume or shorts and a T-shirt. To look less conspicuous in towns, wear long trousers. At night in winter, the temperature drops enough to warrant a light sweater or jacket. In upmarket hotels, restaurants, and nightclubs, men are expected to wear a collared shirt and trousers and women are required to dress equally smartly.

COMMUNICATIONS

Telephones (*teléfono*). Patience is required when using the country's antiquated telephone system which, however, is currently being upgraded. In the meantime, it can take a while to get a connection on an international line outside Havana, and almost as long on a domestic line. You may have to pay a deposit for an outside line from your hotel room. The top hotels have direct-dial facilities for all calls; elsewhere, you can make domestic calls on a direct line, but you will need to go through the hotel's operator for international calls. With the upgrading, many numbers are changing, so ask for help from your hotel if you have trouble getting through to a number.

Domestic and international calls can also be made from telephone centres (*centro telefónico*), located sometimes in the lobbies of large hotels, sometimes in streetside buildings. Some top hotels have card phones, which you can use for all calls; purchase the phone cards from hotel receptions. Pay phones which take pesos (some for local calls only, some for long-distance domestic calls, too) are unreliable. Instructions in Spanish should be posted by the phone.

International calls are expensive. The rate varies little (though hotels may charge for an uncompleted call). Reverse-charge calls are not possible. Hotels charge a significant surcharge on domestic calls.

Cuba

To make an international call from your hotel room, dial 8 or 88 before the country code, and on card phones dial 119. To make a long-distance national call, add the area code (e.g., 07 for Havana). This guide includes area codes in the phone numbers, but elsewhere they are almost always excluded.

Mail. You can buy stamps (*sello*) for dollars at hotels, or for pesos at post offices (*oficina de correos*). The postal system is very unreliable and slow. Postcards (*tarjeta postal*) sent to Europe take about a month to arrive. Mail sent from abroad into Cuba often fails to reach its destination. Moreover, Cubans frequently ask foreigners to post mail on their behalf to friends abroad from abroad.

I want to telephone   **Quiero telefonear a**

England/Canada.   **Inglaterra/Canadá.**

COMPLAINTS

Package holidaymakers with a complaint should seek their company's local representative. If the complaint is serious, make a written and, where appropriate, photographic record, and deliver this to your tour operator as soon as you return home.

As well as asking to see the manager (*jefe/gerente/director*), another course of action which often produces results is to ask for the complaints and suggestions (*quejas y sugerencias*) book.

CRIME   (See also EMERGENCIES on page 113 and POLICE on page 121)

Despite the enormous disparity of wealth between foreigners and locals and a recent increase in crime as the economy has nosedived, Cuba is a safe place to take a holiday. Crime is generally directed at possessions rather than people: place temptation out of sight. Most hotels provide safes, though they usually charge for their use.

City streets at night feel more dangerous than they actually are because they are so poorly lit. The one area where you should be wary of bagsnatchers is in Old Havana, particularly on Calle Obispo and the grid of streets south of it to the train station. Central Havana west of the Prado to the Hotel Deauville also has a bad reputation.

CUSTOMS (*aduana*) **and ENTRY FORMALITIES**

Passports (*pasaporte*). Visitors need a full passport. Its expiry date must not be within six months of your return date from Cuba.

Visas. Tourists need a tourist card (*tarjeta de turista*) to visit Cuba. If you're travelling on a package holiday, the tour operator will arrange your tourist card for you. If travelling independently, contact your country's Cuban embassy. The card is valid for 30 days. If you're planning to stay for longer, the hotel at which you are staying can issue you a new card every month for a period of up to six months. For U.S. formalities, see TRAVELLING TO CUBA on page 126.

Duty-free allowance. Restrictions are as follows into: Cuba: 200 cigarettes or 50 cigars or 250 g tobacco; 2 bottles of spirits; Australia: 250 cigarettes or 250 g tobacco; 1 *l* alcohol; Canada: 200 cigarettes and 50 cigars and 400 g tobacco; 1.14 *l* spirits or wine or 8.5 *l* beer; New Zealand: 200 cigarettes or 50 cigars or 250 g tobacco; 4.5 *l* wine or beer and 1.14 *l* spirits; South Africa: 400 cigarettes and 50 cigars and 250 g tobacco; 2 *l* wine and 1 *l* spirits; U.K.: 200 cigarettes or 50 cigars or 100 cigarillos or 250 g tobacco; 2 *l* still table wine and 1 *l* spirits or an additional 2 *l* of fortified/sparkling wine; U.S.: 200 cigarettes or 50 cigars or a "reasonable amount" of tobacco; 1 *l* wine or spirits. Note that it is illegal to import Cuban cigars as well as any other Cuban product into the United States.

D

DRIVING

Driving conditions. Driving through Cuba is largely blissful as there is so little traffic. Most main roads are tarmacked and in good condition. The Autopista Nacional highway (motorway) runs from Havana west to Pinar del Río, and from Havana east to Sancti Spíritus. It is always eerily empty of traffic and allows you to travel through much of western Cuba at breakneck speed.

However, a number of scenic roads are not paved. Furthermore, always beware of potholes: some are big enough to puncture your tyre and even dent the wheel. As great a hazard are columns of meandering cyclists, and impromptu meetings with sheep, goats, and cows.

Rules of the road. Drive on the right. Don't drink and drive. National speed limits are 100 km/h (60 mph) on the highway (motorway), 90 km/h (55 mph) on other open roads, and 50 km/h (30 mph) in built-up areas. You are liable to get an on-the-spot fine if you're caught breaking the speed limit. Wearing seat belts is not mandatory, though it's wise to do so. Most road signs are internationally understood. It's common practice to hoot your horn when overtaking to let vehicles without rearview mirrors know what's happening.

Fuel (*gasolina*). Only garages owned by the state oil company Cupet can sell fuel to tourists. They are open 24 hours. Car rental companies insist that you use the expensive *especial* petrol (gasoline), though some pump attendants will supply the less expensive *regular*.

Hitchhiking (*coger botella*). For soldiers, teachers, nurses, farmers, schoolchildren — simply for millions of Cubans — hitching is part and parcel of everyday life. Great crowds gather on the outskirts of towns waiting for a lift. Look out for the official in the yellow suit with a clipboard who flags down state vehicles obliged to stop by law. Tourist transport does not have to stop, but you'd be extremely hard-hearted not to do so occasionally. You'll be most unlucky to encounter any difficulties; however, ask at your hotel or the tourist office if it is legal for visitors to pick up locals, as changing laws sometimes forbid the practice.

give way	**Ceda el paso**
caution	**Cuidado**
One way	**Dirección única**
No parking	**No parqueo**
Danger	**Peligro**
Stop	**Pare**

Driving licence	**licencia de manejar**
Full tank please.	**Llénelo, por favor.**
How do I get to...?	**¿Cómo puedo ir a...?**
I have a flat tyre.	**Tengo una llanta desinflada.**
My car has broken down.	**Mi carro se ha descompuesto.**
Are we on the right road for...?	**¿Es ésta la calle que va a...?**

E

ELECTRIC CURRENT

Electrical appliances in hotels operate either on 110v or 220v, and some need flat pin plugs, other round pin plugs — take an adapter; a converter may also be necessary.

EMBASSIES and CONSULATES

Canada: Calle 30 No 518, e/ 5 y 7, Miramar, Havana; tel. (07) 332516/332517/332527/332382/332752.

United Kingdom: Calle 34 No 702/4, e/ 7 y 17, Miramar, Havana; tel. (07) 331771/331772/331286/331299/331049. The U.K. embassy also represents New Zealand interests, and will help Australian and Irish citizens in an emergency.

United States Interests Section: Calzada e/ L y M, Vedado, Havana; tel. (07) 333543 to 47 or (07) 333551 to 59. From a traveller's viewpoint, this office, in the Swiss Embassy, acts in the same way as an American embassy.

EMERGENCIES (See also MEDICAL CARE on page 117 and POLICE on page 121)

Asistur is a state-run organization which helps foreigners with medical or financial problems and is affiliated to a number of international travel insurance companies. For a 10% commission and if provided with bank details overseas, they can negotiate a cash advance. They can also help with the retrieval of lost luggage and the issue of travel documents. Asistur's office is at Paseo del Prado No 254, e/ Animas y Trocadero, Habana Vieja; tel. (07) 338527/625519/ 638284. It also has offices in Varadero, Cienfuegos, and Santiago.

Here are some useful numbers and phrases:

Police	116
Fire brigade	115

There is no single emergency number for the ambulance service.

fire	**fuego**
Help!	**¡Socorro!**
Look out!	**¡Cuidado!**
Stop thief!	**¡Al ladrón!**

ENVIRONMENTAL ISSUES

You may be tempted to buy exotic souvenirs for you and your family on your holiday, but spare a thought for endangered plants and animals which may be threatened by your purchase. Even trade in tourist souvenirs can threaten the most endangered species.

More than 800 species of animals and plants are currently banned from international trade by CITES (Convention on International Trade in Endangered Species and Plants). These include many corals, shells, cacti, orchids, and hardwoods, as well as the more obvious turtles. So think twice before you buy — it may be illegal, and your souvenirs could be confiscated by Customs on your return.

For further information or a fact sheet contact the following:

U.K. — Department of the Environment; tel. (0117) 987-8961 (birds, reptiles and fish), or (0117) 9878168 (plants and mammals).

United States — Fish and Wildlife Service; tel. (703) 358-2095.

Canada — Canadian Wildlife Service; tel. (819) 953-1404/997-1840.

ETIQUETTE

Cubans are generally fun-loving, sensuous people, and for many visitors friendships with Cubans will constitute the highlight of their stay. However, less gregarious holidaymakers can find the locals' constant badgering very wearying. Cubans find it hard to understand unsociable people, and there's no easy solution to fending off unwanted attention. A courteous smile and a *"no gracias"* (no thanks) to any advance is the simplest advice.

While you should by no means be put off entering into friendships, at the same time realize that however genuine your Cuban friends are, they may well be pursuing some economic agenda: Cubans are very poor in comparison with foreigners, who are universally seen as walking money banks. Initially when people approach you, it's often not clear what exactly they want. They may just be hoping for a few free beers and a square meal, or they may ask for dollars, or for T-shirts, soap, or any other accoutrement which only dollars can buy. They may try to offer black-market cigars and rum, to sell you accommodation at someone's home, and to change your dollars for pesos at an inflated black-market rate. The sale of all these things is illegal. Kids, meanwhile, shriek *"chicle"* (chewing-gum), *"pluma"* (pen), and *"moneda"* (coin) at every turn. Many tourists therefore bring a stash of pens, T-shirts, chewing-gum, and bars of soap to give away, and leave behind unused toiletries and medicines as presents.

L

LANGUAGE

Although young Cubans now learn English at school and old Cubans used English frequently before the revolution, many people, especially away from the resorts, do not speak English at all.

good/bad	**bueno/malo**
yesterday/today/tomorrow	**ayer/hoy/mañana**
Hello.	**Hola.**

Cuba

Good night	**Buenos noches**
I'm thirsty/hungry	**Teno sed/hambre**
Until later	**hasta luego**

The Berlitz *Latin-American Spanish Phrase Book and Dictionary* includes over 1,200 phrases and an explanation of how Latin-American Spanish varies in its pronunciation from Castilian Spanish.

M

MAPS

There are no detailed road maps of Cuba. The best maps (not on sale in Cuba and both slightly out of date) are Hildebrand's *Urlaubskarte Cuba* (1:1100000), and Freytag & Berndts *Kuba/Cuba* (1:1250 000), which is less up-to-date but has useful city plans. Of Cuba's metropolitan areas, only Havana and Santiago are too large to explore without a map (essential to avoid getting lost while driving through Havana's suburbs). Hotels and bookshops in both cities sell reasonable maps.

MEDIA

Radio. Radio Taíno (1160 AM), a tourist-oriented music station with some broadcasts in English, is most easily heard around Havana. Tune in to the American Forces Network around Guantánamo on 102.1 FM and 103.1 FM for insights into life in the U.S. naval base.

Newspapers and magazines (*periódico; revista*). Press freedom is severely restricted, and newspapers are difficult to find, particularly outside Havana. The main national newspaper, *Granma*, is often filled with Castro's lengthy speeches, but it's interesting to read about Cuba's official view of itself. A weekly *Granma International* is published in English, French, and German, with cultural features of tourist appeal. Other national newspapers include the weekly *Trabajadores* (Workers) and *Juventud Rebelde* (Rebel Youth). *Bohemia*, a respected monthly magazine founded in 1908, has in-depth analyses of contemporary Cuba and the world as seen through Cuban eyes.

For tourist-oriented information in Spanish and English, in Havana look for the weekly Havana listings magazine *Cartelera*, with details on theatrical events, cabarets, and gallery exhibitions, and the listings booklet *La Habana*. In Santiago, the monthly *Guía Caribeña* magazine has cultural articles and listings.

MEDICAL CARE (see also EMERGENCIES on page 113)

Vaccinations. There are no mandatory vaccinations required for travelling to Cuba, but vaccinations against typhoid, tetanus, polio, and Hepatitis A are recommended.

Staying healthy. The most likely source of food poisoning is from unhygienic hotel buffet food. As Cuban food is very plain, upset stomachs are less common than in many other undeveloped countries.

The Cuban sun can burn fair-skinned people within minutes. Use plenty of sun cream and wear a hat. It's also easy to become dehydrated, so be sure to drink plenty of water.

From dusk to dawn in coastal resorts, mosquitoes are a menace. Air-conditioning helps keep them at bay, but apply insect repellent.

As far as beach safety is concerned, a few resort beaches employ a flag system indicating if swimming is safe. A red flag means no swimming, a yellow flag take care, and a green flag safe swimming. Don't scuba dive less than 24 hours prior to flying.

Treatment. If you need to see a doctor, contact your hotel's reception. Large resort hotels have their own doctor. All the island's main resorts have an international clinic (*clínica internacional*), as does Havana, Santiago de Cuba, Cienfuegos, and Trinidad. Medical treatment in Cuba is excellent and free for Cubans. Foreigners, however, must pay, and treatment is expensive, so proper insurance is essential.

Pharmacies. Every town has an all-night pharmacy (*farmacia*). The range of medicines has become severely limited in recent years. Resorts have better-stocked international pharmacists, though prices can be astronomical, so bring all the medicines you might need during your stay, including mosquito repellent and insect-bite cream.

Cuba

hospital	**hospital**
Call a doctor/dentist.	**Llame a un médico/dentista.**

MONEY MATTERS (See also CUSTOMS and ENTRY FORMALITIES on page 111)

Currency. Two currencies operate in Cuba, the U.S. dollar (*dólar* or *divisa*, literally "hard currency") and the peso. Confusingly, prices in shops are displayed as $ for both currencies, with U.S. dollars also marked as USD to differentiate. The peso has no international value and, as Cuba is desperate for hard currency, virtually everything tourists can buy — accommodation, food, drink, transport, souvenirs — is sold in dollars. Since dollar notes are in short supply, something called the "convertible peso" has recently been introduced. This is interchangeable with, and has the same value as, the dollar. As convertible pesos have no value outside Cuba, you are allowed to change any you still hold at the end of your trip for dollars.

If you change dollars for pesos in a bank or hotel currency exchange, you'll be given one peso per dollar (on leaving the country you can change a paltry maximum of 10 normal pesos into dollars, and only if you have the receipt for their original purchase). However, on the black market (*bolsa negra* or *mercado negro*) on which much of the economy operates, one dollar has remained consistently worth around 40 pesos since the mid-1990s. Changing money on the black market, though a widespread practice, is illegal. Furthermore, it is extremely difficult to spend any significant amount of pesos. Just about all you can or would want to buy with them are stamps, fruit from markets, and perhaps a beer or rum in a local bar. Even if a restaurant or bar accepts pesos, as a foreigner you may have to pay in dollars.

It used to be illegal for Cubans to own or spend dollars. This policy was abandoned in 1993 in an attempt to bring into the official economy the millions of dollars swilling around the black market economy. Now Cubans can spend their greenbacks in the rash of newly opened dollar-only shops in every town, and many restaurants and bars serving locals have started to charge in dollars, too.

Traveller's cheques (*cheque de viaje*). Come with dollar traveller's cheques. On account of the political situation between Cuba and the United States, American Express traveller's cheques are not accepted. The easiest way to change traveller's cheques into dollars is at hotels. Commission rates vary from 2% to 4%. Ask for notes in denominations of $20 or less, since few establishments can change $50 or $100 notes. If you've mistakenly arrived in Cuba with American Express traveller's cheques, Asistur (see EMERGENCIES, page 113) can cash them for a 10% commission.

Credit cards (*tarjeta de crédito*). American Express is not accepted anywhere, nor is any credit card issued in the United States. Most tourist shops, as well as upmarket hotels and restaurants, airlines, and car rental companies, accept other major credit cards. For large credit card payments, you will be asked to show your passport.

PLANNING YOUR BUDGET

To give you an idea of what to expect, here are some guidelines as to prices. Prices vary greatly from one establishment to the next.

Accommodation. See the introduction to the Recommended Hotels starting on page 130 for an indication of general price bands.

Bicycle rental. $2 an hour, $12 a day.

Cabaret. From $30 at Havana's Tropicana, $15 at smaller venues.

Car rental. For an economy car with unlimited mileage, from $45 a day, $280 a week. $5–15 a day extra for insurance. Examples of drop-off charges: pick up Havana, leave in Varadero $35; pick up Havana, leave in Guantánamo $162.

Cigars. Boxes of 25 cigars: Montecristo No. 4 (5-inch) $45; Cohiba Lancero (7 1/2-inch) $250.

Organized excursions. From Havana, a two-day, one-night trip to: Santiago $200, Cayo Largo $169. From Varadero, a day trip to: Havana $38, Cayo Largo $94, Trinidad $89, Santiago $118.

Cuba

Internal flights. One-way flights (returns are usually exactly double): Havana–Santiago $68, Havana–Holguin $60, Havana–Nueva Gerona (Isle of Youth) $17.

Meals and drinks. Breakfast $4–7; light lunch $10; restaurant dinner $10–25; lobster $25; hotel dinner buffets $15–25; bottle of beer $1–2; bottle of wine from $10; cocktail $2–3.

Mopeds. $9 per hour, $15 for three hours.

Museums. $1–3.

Petrol (gasoline). 90 cents per litre.

Spirits. Bottle of: 3-year-old rum $5, 7-year-old rum $8.

Taxis. 65 cents–$1 per kilometre. Central Havana to airport $13–16, Old Havana to Vedado $4.

Telephone calls. Per minute, $2.50–4 to North America and Central America, $4.50–5 to South America, $5.50–6.50 to rest of the world. From a hotel, long-distance national calls per minute: $1–2.75; local calls 20–50 cents.

Trains. $35 single Havana-Santiago.

Watersports. Diving: certificated 5-day course $350; introduction, with two dives $110; one dive $25–35. Waterskiing: $1 per minute.

O

OPENING HOURS (see also PUBLIC HOLIDAYS on page 122)

Offices. Usually open weekdays from 8am to 5pm, with a one-hour lunch break. Some are open on Saturday mornings, too.

Banks. Typically open weekdays from 8:30am to 3pm.

Museums. A few open daily, but most close for one whole day (usually but not always Monday) and on Sunday at noon or 1pm. Typical opening times are 9am (sometimes 8am or 10am) to 5pm (sometimes

4pm or 6pm). Many are closed for renovations: make inquiries before travelling a long way.

Restaurants. Hotel restaurants usually shut around 9:30pm. More modest restaurants often stop serving earlier, as they run out of food.

Shops. Tourist shops usually open from 10am to 6 or 7pm daily. For main street shops, those selling essential goods such as food tend to open from 9am to 5 or 6pm Monday to Saturday, while those selling things like books tend to open from noon to 6 or 7pm.

P

PHOTOGRAPHY and VIDEO

Buy in your home country all the film and camera equipment you might need. A limited range of film is available in hotel shops and shops called Photoservice; video cassettes are very hard to come by.

You are not allowed to photograph military installations, certain factories, or civilian airports: if in doubt, ask first. Many museums prohibit the taking of photographs or charge a fee. The Tropicana in Havana charges, too (including a hefty fee for video filming). Use a faster film to increase the distance the flash works.

Cuban people are wonderfully photogenic and usually like having their photo taken, but of course, it's polite to ask first. Some may ask for a dollar in return.

For handy tips on how to get the most out of your holiday snaps, be sure to purchase a copy of the Berlitz-Nikon *Pocket Guide to Travel Photography* (available in the U.K. only).

POLICE (policía)

Most Cuban police are friendlier than they might appear as they slouch over their motorbikes, sporting shades and moustaches. Those bearing labels marking them as special tourist police should speak a foreign language. Some tourists find the ubiquitous presence of the police outside hotels in Havana and Varadero disconcerting; others may find it reassuring.

You should bear in mind that locals are very sensitive about the possibility of plain-clothes state security agents overhearing them voice dissent against the system, or even just seeing them forging close friendships with foreigners.

Where's the police station?	**¿Dónde está la comisaría de policía?**

PUBLIC HOLIDAYS *(día festivo)*

The following days are public holidays in Cuba.

January 1	Anniversary of the Triumph of the Revolution, Liberation Day
May 1	International Workers' Day
July 25-27	National Rebellion Day (July 26)
October 10	Beginning of the Wars of Independence

R

RELIGION

Syncretic religions like Santería (see page 35) are more dominant in Cuba than Catholicism. Government measures heavily blunted the power and influence of the Catholic church in the early 1960s (for example, by abolishing religious holidays). Mass, however, is still said in numerous churches throughout the island, and there are many Protestant churches, too.

T

TIME DIFFERENCES

Cuba is 5 hours behind GMT. It operates on Eastern Standard Time in winter and Daylight Savings Time (one hour later) from April to October.

Cuba	Montreal	New York	London	Sydney
noon	noon	noon	5pm	3am

TIPPING *(propina)*

Wherever you go as a tourist — even in shops, toilets, garages, car parks — tipping is expected. In hotels and restaurants, tips are shared out among all staff (though direct recipients get the lion's share). In a typical evening, barmen and waiters earn in dollar tips the peso equivalent of two month's wages. As a result, linguistics professors and research scientists clean dining-tables and serve cocktails. A tip of 10% in restaurants and taxis is expected, and loose change at a bar. Tour guides expect at least a couple of dollars for their services, and roving musical groups should be given a dollar. In almost any other situation, a dollar is a very generous tip, and loose change may be more appropriate.

TOILETS *(baños/servicios)*

Put a toilet roll in the bottom of your bag when you're out and about in Cuba. Establishments do not always provide their own toilet paper.

TOURIST INFORMATION

Canada: Cuba Tourist Board, 55 Queen Street East, Suite 705, Toronto, Ontario M5C 1R6; tel. (416) 362-0700.

U.K.: Cuba Ministry of Tourism, 167 High Holborn, London WC1V 6PA; tel. (0171) 3791706.

In Cuba, all hotels have a tourism desk *(buro de turismo)*. They are primarily geared towards selling excursions, but should also provide information about museums, restaurants, and so forth. Also useful in Havana are Infotur offices for dealing with queries about the city. Infotur offices in Old Havana can be found on the Parque Central by the Hotel Plaza, and on Calle Obispo number 306 and number 358. Otherwise, Cuba's tourism industry is very complex. The three companies you most frequently come across are Cubatur, Havanatur, and Cubanacán, who make excursions, transfers, and so forth on behalf of foreign tour operators.

If you need a particular address or phone number, ask to see the *Directorio Turistico de Cuba* (the Cuban Tourist Directory).

TOURS

The most popular and straightforward way of exploring Cuba is on group excursions. However, these trips, led by carefully vetted tour

123

guides, insulate you from many of the most interesting aspects of Cuban life. You can reach virtually the whole island from any resort on excursions. Some involve a short trip to the nearby town and its tobacco factory. Others begin with a long coach journey or a flight to one of the island's showpiece colonial towns or chief cities; often you can choose between staying overnight or making a day trip. Many boat and even helicopter trips take you to pristine beaches on offshore islands.

TRANSPORT (See also BICYCLE AND MOPED HIRE on page 106, CAR HIRE on page 107, DRIVING on page 111, and TOURS on page 123)

With hundreds of people stuffed like sardines into buses and a return to horse-drawn vehicles, Cuba's sorry public transport system is perhaps the clearest manifestation of the country's economic woes.

Domestic flights. Flying in Cuba is by far the quickest and most reliable form of transport. It's also good value. Flights fill up fast, so book in advance from your home country where possible. Cubana, the national airline, provides most domestic flights, including those from Havana to Baracoa, Bayamo, Camagüey, Cayo Largo, Ciego de Ávila, Cienfuegos, Guantánamo, Holguín, Nueva Gerona (Isle of Youth), Manzanillo, Santiago, and Varadero. Frequency varies enormously, from five a day to Santiago to two a week to Baracoa.

Flights generally leave on time, if not early. Check in at least an hour before the departure time to avoid losing your seat. The planes are rickety old things; the smoke-like emissions of prehistoric air-conditioning systems can be disturbing for first-time Cubana users. Tickets can also be purchased in Cubana offices around the country or from its head office on Calle 23 (La Rampa) No 64, e/ P y Infanta, tel. (07) 334949 to 96. Cubana also has an office in Canada: Cubanacan International Canada, 372 Bay Street, Suite 1902, Toronto, Ontario M5H 2W9; tel. (416) 601-0343. Agencies use the charter airline Aerocaribbean for excursions on many routes. Its Havana office is virtually next to Cubana's head office; tel. (07) 797524.

Buses (*guaguas*) provide the backbone of Cuba's public transport system. However, they are presently few and far between, and usually impossibly full when they do arrive.

The length of time you have to wait at bus stops has been reduced a little by the recent introduction of *tren* buses, nicknamed *camellos* (camels) — lorry-pulled colossuses which can carry 300 people. Further deterrents for tourists using buses come in the form of complicated ticketing methods and the confusing array of separate local, provincial, and inter-provincial services.

Taxis (*taxis*) are ubiquitous wherever tourists congregate. All are metered and you must pay in dollars (tourists cannot use peso taxis). Hiring a taxi for the day is more expensive than hiring a car, but with a full complement of passengers to share the cost it can be affordable.

In the main cities, private car owners offer rides at cut-price dollar rates. This is illegal, and drivers, if caught, will be imprisoned and fined; foreigners will just be cautioned. Drivers therefore encourage passengers to pretend they are just friends and that no financial transaction is taking place. The most alluring reason for taking a ride is the opportunity to cruise around in the back of an old Cadillac.

Horse-and-traps/carriages (*coches*). Due to fuel shortages, in virtually every city except Havana and Santiago, horses pull traps and plush little carriages up and down the main streets. Sometimes the vehicles ply set routes and take all comers, sometimes you'll find them acting as taxis. Ironically, horse-and-traps have become a tourist attraction in the resorts.

Trains (*trens*). Few tourists travel by train. The journeys are extremely slow (16 hours from Havana to Santiago, for example) and schedules are unreliable. However, the stations and trains themselves are wonderfully atmospheric. Those who pay in dollars can travel in comfort and make bookings through Ferrotur offices located at train stations (Havana, tel. 07 621770; Santiago, tel. 07 22254). You're advised to collect your ticket two hours before you travel. The one service of real potential interest to tourists is the overnight train from Havana to Santiago and Santiago to Havana on alternate days, stopping on the way at most of central Cuba's chief towns.

TRAVELLERS WITH DISABILITIES

Travel in Cuba for people with disabilities is tough. Even Cuba's new luxury hotels rarely have proper facilities for travellers with disabilities. If you're travelling on a package, discuss your requirements in as much detail as possible with your tour operator before booking.

TRAVELLING TO CUBA (See also AIRPORTS on page 106)

From Canada. Most flights to Cuba leave from Montreal or Toronto, taking around four hours. There are also departures from Halifax and Ottawa. Except for a weekly scheduled departure from Montreal to Havana, all flights are charters. They arrive at Havana, Varadero, Cayo Largo, Cienfuegos (for Zapata, Rancho Luna, Trinidad), Ciego de Ávila (for Cayo Coco), Camagüey (for Playa Santa Lucía), Holguín (for Guardalavaca), Manzanillo (for Marea del Portillo), and Santiago (for Parque Baconoa).

From the U.K. Scheduled flights leave from London to Havana via Spain, Holland, and Venezuela. But Cubana's weekly service to Havana (via Newfoundland to refuel, returning direct) is normally the least expensive and quickest (12 hours outbound, 9 hours inbound), and also includes the offer of a free return domestic flight. There are also charter flights to Varadero and Camagüey (for Playa Santa Lucía and Guardalavaca).

From the U.S. Because of the U.S. trade embargo, the U.S. government does not allow its citizens to spend money in Cuba except in special circumstances — as a result, U.S. citizens are not allowed to travel directly to Cuba from the U.S. without special permission, but are free to enter Cuba from a third country. Those wishing to travel officially should seek permission from the Licensing Division, Office of Foreign Assets Control, 1500 Pennsylvania Avenue NW, Washington, DC 20220 tel. (202) 622-2480, before contacting the Cuban Interests Section in Washington, DC for a visa. If you succeed in getting a visa, you can take the regular flight from Miami to Havana; phone Marazul Tours (305) 885-6161 or (800) 223-5334.

Package holidays. Most tourists opt for a fortnight's package holiday and stay in one resort. Twin-centre resort packages are possible too, often featuring a second week in Cayo Largo. Cultural holidays are also popular. Typically, these involve a week or fortnight-long coach tour around the island, staying in places such as Havana, Viñales, Trinidad, Santiago, and Baracoa, and maybe including visits to hospitals and cooperative farms. Such tours offer the most hassle-free and affordable way of seeing a large proportion of Cuba. Contact the Cuban tourist office in your home country (see TOURIST INFORMATION on page 123) for a list of tour operators.

Independent travel. Tourism in Cuba is geared towards package holidaymakers, but there's nothing to stop you travelling independently. If you do, you'll have much more contact with local people. Adventurousness, patience to deal with administrative hassles, and at least a willingness to speak some Spanish are all you need.

Some independent travellers use a specialist travel company in their home country to book accommodation and car rental. In Cuba, the local agency that works with your specialist company issues you with a voucher for each booking, so that (in theory) when you arrive at a hotel or car rental office and produce the relevant voucher, the establishment readily acknowledges your reservation and payment. You can also travel to Cuba without any reservations, giving you plenty of freedom and plenty of potential administrative problems. It's best to make bookings in your home country for at least the first and last nights of your stay, and for internal flights.

W

WATER

Though Cuban water is chlorinated, standards have deteriorated recently, so you're advised against drinking tap water where possible. Mineral water (*agua mineral*) is widely available.

WEIGHTS AND MEASURES

Cuba uses the metric system, with metres, kilometres, litres, and kilograms. The only non-metric unit that is still occasionally used is the livre, a pound of weight.

Cuba

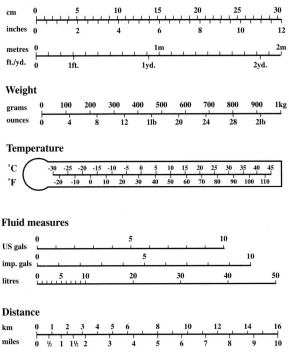

Length

cm	0	5	10	15	20	25	30
inches	0	2	4	6	8	10	12

metres	0	1m	2m
ft./yd.	0	1ft.	1yd.	2yd.

Weight

grams	0	100	200	300	400	500	600	700	800	900	1kg
ounces	0	4	8	12	1lb	20	24	28	2lb		

Temperature

°C	-30 -25 -20 -15 -10 -5 0 5 10 15 20 25 30 35 40 45
°F	-20 -10 0 10 20 30 40 50 60 70 80 90 100 110

Fluid measures

US gals	0	5	10
imp. gals	0	5	10
litres	0	5	10	20	30	40	50

Distance

km	0 1 2 3 4 5 6 8 10 12 14 16
miles	0 ½ 1 1½ 2 3 4 5 6 7 8 9 10

WOMEN TRAVELLERS

Female foreigners, like male foreigners, are likely to receive plenty of unsolicited attention, but normally of a genuinely friendly nature. Cuba is a relatively unthreatening and safe place for women travellers.

A SELECTION OF HOTELS AND RESTAURANTS

Recommended Hotels

The following selection should help those on a package choose a hotel from tour operators' brochures. For those travelling independently, the recommendations cover hotels in all corners of the island, including, where there is no better alternative, those which are only recommendable for their useful location. Even if you've already chosen your hotel, some establishments are worth visiting for their architecture, ambience, bars, and restaurants. All hotels have a pool unless otherwise stated.

The price bands below are for a standard room for two people per night in high season, excluding all meals, and are in U.S. dollars. If you're not travelling on a package, prepare to pay with dollars in cash or with dollar traveller's cheques. Top hotels accept credit cards — but remember, credit cards issued by American Express or American banks are not accepted in Cuba.

High season is from mid-December to mid-April and from July to August. Prices drop by 15% to 35% during other months.

✪	under $45
✪✪	$45 – 80
✪✪✪	$80 – 120
✪✪✪✪	over $120

OLD HAVANA

Inglaterra ✪✪✪ *Prado No. 416, esq. San Rafael; Habana Vieja; Tel. (07) 338593 to 99; fax (07) 338254.* The city's most historic hotel was founded in 1875. Its ornately tiled and stuccoed bar and restaurant is a great meeting place, while its open-air rooftop bar has live music weekend evenings. Best bedrooms face the Parque Central, but many of the 83 rooms are pokey and some even windowless. No pool.

Plaza ✪✪✪ *Zulueta y Neptuno; Habana Vieja;.* Tel. (07) 338583; fax (07) 338591/333892. Heavily restored, turn-of-the-century hotel on the Parque Central with very elegant public rooms and high-quality bedrooms. No pool but residents can always use the pool at the nearby Sevilla (see below). 186 rooms.

Sevilla ✪✪✪✪ *Trocadero e/ Zulueta y Prado; Habana Vieja;* Tel. (07) 338580; fax (07) 338582. Recently restored 1920s establishment, now the best in Old Havana. Highly sumptuous lobby, magnificent stuccoed rooftop restaurant, and other excellent dining options such as a Spanish restaurant, as well as a gallery of stylish shops. Good pool, gymnasium. 192 comfortable rooms.

Hostal Valencia ✪ *Oficios No.53 e/ Lamparilla y Obrapía; Habana Vieja;* Tel. (07) 623801. Far and away the best budget option in Havana and with the best location of any hotel in the city, just 200 metres (600 feet) from the Plaza de Armas. The 18th-century mansion has 14 rooms arranged around an attractive courtyard, an atmospheric bar, and decent Spanish restaurant serving good food. You need to book well in advance. No pool.

NEW HAVANA

Deauville ✪✪ *Galiano y Malecón; Centro Habana;* Tel. (07) 628051-59; fax (07) 338148. An ugly tower-block hotel, but set right on the seafront. Big rooms (a large number with ocean-facing balconies), good breakfasts, and a lively disco. A 10-minute walk into Old Havana. 148 rooms.

Meliá Cohiba ✪✪✪✪ *Paseo e/ 1ra y 3r; Vedado;* Tel. (07) 336245/336246; fax (07) 334555. This brand-new, business-oriented establishment is Cuba's most expensive place to stay and has all the trappings of a top international chain hotel. Its location in western Vedado is not ideal for tourists. Attractions for non-residents include a cigar bar. 462 rooms.

Nacional de Cuba ✪✪✪✪ *Calle O esq. 21; Vedado;* Tel. (07) 333564/333567; fax (07) 335054 or (07) 335171. This long-established, landmark hotel on the waterfront was where

Wormold was nearly poisoned in *Our Man in Havana*. The cuisine is considerably better now. Stunning dining-room, excellent buffet dinner, two pools, nightly cabaret, gardens, attractive terraces, and stylish bars. 488 rooms.

Victoria ✪✪✪ *Calle 19 y M; Vedado; Tel. (07) 333510; fax (07) 333109.* Stylish, quiet hotel catering principally for businesspeople, close to Vedado's main street, La Rampa. Attentive staff. 31 slick bedrooms.

PINAR DEL RÍO PROVINCE

La Ermita ✪ *Carretera de la Ermita Km 2; Viñales; Tel. (08) 93204; fax (08) 936091.* Just a short, enjoyable walk from Viñales town and with fine valley views, this modern, low-rise complex is in other respects less seductive than nearby Los Jazmines. 62 rooms.

Los Jazmines ✪ *Carretera de Viñales Km 25 (2 km from Viñales); Tel. (08) 93205; fax (08) 335042.* An unimpeded panorama of Viñales' stupendously beautiful valley from every balcony of the 48 fetching bedrooms and from the terrace around the excellent pool. Good food and friendly, welcoming management.

Moka ✪✪ *Communidad Las Terrazas; Candelaria (turn right off motorway at 51 km mark from Havana); Tel. and fax (085) 335516.* A seductive, gleaming new complex in a gorgeously peaceful, lush setting in the eastern foothills of Pinar del Río's mountains. 26 very comfortable bedrooms with imaginative bathrooms. Nature tours by bike and on horseback.

ISLE OF YOUTH

El Colony ✪✪ *Carretera de Siguanea Km 16; Tel. (061) 9818.* Situated on the coast approximately 42 km (26 miles) southwest of Nueva Gerona, this is an isolated, overpriced 1950s tourist enclave of exclusive interest to divers. The hotel itself and its beach are unappealing, but the 83 bedrooms are comfortably equipped.

Villa Gaviota ✪ *Autopista Nueva Gerona; La Fé Km 1; Tel. (061) 23290.* Modest but well-maintained riverside complex set around a decent pool, just outside Nueva Gerona. 23 spacious, modern rooms.

CAYO LARGO

Isla del Sur ✪✪✪; also **Villa Capricho, Villa Iguana, Villa Coral** *Tel. (095)794215; fax (095) 333156.* Four adjacent beachside complexes share comprehensive leisure facilities, but each offering guests its own style of accommodation. The most romantic is Villa Capricho, with 60 vaulted, thatched bungalows set amid mangroves and palms, all thoughtfully equipped with a hammock strung across the threshold. Villa Coral, with 72 rooms spread through small villas around an enticing pool, is the most stylish.

VARADERO

Club Kawama ✪✪ *Reparto Kawama; Tel. (05) 667155/667156; fax (05) 667004.* Towards the western end of the resort, a mix of 34 old and modern villas spaciously arranged around pleasant gardens. Direct access to the beach and a lively beach bar, but no pool. 205 simple but pleasant, shuttered rooms.

Cuatro Palmas ✪✪✪✪ *Avenida 1ra e/ 61 y 62; Tel. (05) 63912; fax (05) 667208.* An attractive, upmarket beachside complex situated right in the centre of the resort. Some of the 309 rooms (which can be a little worn) are arranged around an excellent palmy pool, while others lie in bungalows.

Internacional ✪✪✪ *Carretera Las Américas; Tel. (05) 667038; fax (05) 667246.* Varadero's renowned 1950s hotel still has plenty of style, particularly in its restaurants and nightlife: its buffet dinners and Cabaret Continental (see page 90) are the best in town. Huge range of facilities. 371 rooms divided between bungalows in gardens and large rooms overlooking the beach.

Meliá Las Américas ✪✪✪✪ *Carretera Las Morlas; Playa Las Américas; Tel. (05) 337600; fax (05) 337625.* This Spanish-run hotel matches its neighbour, the Meliá Varadero, for quality and facilities. Las Américas is newer, smaller (290 rooms in pretty colours), and more demure, with live classical music in its foyer and good food.

Meliá Varadero ✪✪✪✪ *Autopista del Sur; Playa Las Américas; Tel. (05) 337013; fax (05) 337012.* A dazzling complex at the resort's far eastern end. A fountained atrium, vast pool, three good restaurants (one with a fine buffet) and sophisticated shops. 490 rooms, each with a sofa and most with good views. Direct beach access.

Villa Caleta ✪✪ *Calle 19 e/ 1ra y Playa; Tel. (05) 63515.* Modest hotel near the resort's centre, focused around a rustic pool. 46 rattan-furnished rooms, some in little apartment blocks and with balconies overlooking the beach, others more spacious but suffering from traffic noise.

ZAPATA PENINSULA

Villa Guamá ✪ *Laguna del Tesoro; Ciénaga de Zapata; Tel. (059) 2979.* One of the most distinctive places to stay in Cuba and reachable only by boat. Reasonably equipped thatched huts are spread over a series of interconnected islands in the middle of a swamp. Be warned that mosquito repellent is essential. 34 rooms.

Villa Hotels Playa Larga ✪ *Playa Larga; Ciénaga de Zapata; Tel. (059) 7219.* Low-key complex comprising spacious yet simple bungalows, in grassy parkland by a decent beach at the northern end of the Bay of Pigs. No pool. 49 rooms.

CIENFUEGOS

Jagua ✪✪ *Calle 37 No. 1; Punta Gorda; Tel. (0432) 6302.* An ugly 1950s building, but in a good position just south of the city centre on the edge of the bay, and with reasonable facilities, including a nightly cabaret. 145 comfortable rooms.

Hotel Horizontes Rancho Luna ✪ *Carretera Rancho Luna Km 16; Tel. (0432) 5292.* A rather scruffy, low-rise complex catering to package holidaymakers, 16 km (10 miles) to the east of Cienfuegos. Situated, nonetheless, next to an attractive little beach. 225 rooms.

TRINIDAD

Ancón ✪✪ *Playa Ancón; Tel. (0419) 4011/3155; fax (0419) 337424.* 14 km (9 miles) from Trinidad, an ugly high-rise block beside an excellent beach, equipped with comprehensive watersports facilities. Car, moped, and bicycle hire compensate for the hotel's isolated position. 279 rooms.

Las Cuevas ✪ *Finca Santa Ana; Tel. (0419) 4013; fax (0419) 2302.* The only hotel within easy walking distance (15 minutes) of the centre of Trinidad. Simple, relatively modern bungalows laid out across a hillside and with a decent pool. 124 rooms.

Casa del Campesino ✪ *Finca Maria Dolores, Carretera Circuito Sur; Tel. (0419) 3581.* 3 km (2 miles) west of Trinidad, 20 flower-bedecked bungalows set in a mango orchard next to a river (no pool). Geese and horses graze peacefully nearby (horse riding is on offer). Rustic cabarets in the thatched restaurant.

SIERRA DEL ESCAMBRAY

Hotel Hanabanilla ✪ *Lago Hanabanillal; Manicaragua; Tel. (042) 49125.* 23 km (14 miles) to the west of Manicaragua, a large, unattractive concrete block in a lovely lakeside setting. Fishing and boat trips are available. Cubans outnumber foreigners in the reasonably comfortable 125 rooms.

SANCTI SPÍRITUS

Zaza ✪✪ *Finca San Jose, Lago Zaza; Tel. (041) 26021; fax (041) 66800.* A few miles east of Sancti Spíritus town, a Soviet-style block pleasantly sited by a lake. Decent food. 128 simple rooms.

CAYO COCO AND AROUND

Club Cayo Guillermo ✪✪✪ *Cayo Guillermo; Tel. (07) 301012/301160; fax (07) 335221.* A sizeable resort hotel used almost exclusively by Italians. 212 quality rooms in bungalows

---

and villas. Comprehensive range of facilities, especially water-sports, and a picturesque beach.

Guitart Cayo Coco ✪✪✪✪ *Cayo Coco; Tel. (07) 335384; fax (07) 335166.* Cuba's most attractive resort hotel, amid palmy gardens and alongside a dazzling beach, consists of pastel-coloured villas interwoven by a magnificent sculpted pool. Excellent staff, a cornucopia of watersports, no fewer than six restaurants with good food, first-rate shops. 458 colourful rooms.

Cubanacán Morón ✪✪ *Avenida Tarafa; Morón; Tel. (0335) 3901 to 3905.* Above-average, Soviet-style hotel situated on the edge of Morón, with a restaurant serving reasonably tasty food and with 144 stylish bedrooms.

CAMAGÜEY

Cubanacán Maraguan ✪✪ *Circunvalación Este; Tel. (0332) 72017/72170.* 10 km (6 miles) east of Camagüey, a former country club in a rural spot. 35 simple rooms, mostly in bungalows. Fine large pool and excellent staff. Remnants of a 1960s Soviet missile site lurk in the undergrowth nearby.

PLAYA SANTA LUCÍA

Golden Tulip Club Caracol ✪✪ *Tel. (032) 36302; fax (032) 335043.* The resort's prettiest hotel has floral gardens, art for sale, and neat, modern villas that comprise 150 fancy bedrooms, each with a balcony and sitting area. Full range of activities and facilities.

Cuatro Vientos ✪✪ *Tel. (032) 236160; fax (032) 335433.* A new hotel with 203 rooms in thatched villas spread through landscaped gardens, and expanding. Good buffet food, appealing pool, a full timetable of activities and impressively furnished bedrooms.

GUARDALAVACA

Las Brisas Club Resort ✪✪✪ *Playa Guardalavaca; Tel. (024) 30218; fax (024) 335562.* This new Canadian venture offers a choice of candlelit restaurants with good food, an attractive pool, direct beach access, watersports, and enthusiastic in-house entertainment. 231 rooms.

Río de Luna ✪✪✪ *Playa Estero Ciego; Tel. (024) 30202; fax (024) 30126.* A quiet hotel for package holidaymakers, 4 km (2½ miles) west of Guardalavaca above a good beach. Afternoon tea sets the tone. 222 large, well-furnished rooms.

Guardalavaca Villa ✪ *Playa Guardalavaca; Tel. (024) 30212.* A budget option, near the beach with just a bar and restaurant. 24 simple rooms, each with a terrace.

BAYAMO

Sierra Maestra ✪ *Carretera de Bayamo Km 7.5; Tel. (023) 481013.* A Soviet-style complex some 2 km (1 mile) from the centre of town, with no charm but decent facilities. Amusing poolside cabarets at the weekends. 202 rooms.

SIERRA MAESTRA

Farallon del Caribe ✪✪ *Playa Marea del Portillo; Tel. (023) 594032 to 37.* A Canadian-managed hotel just a few hundred yards from the beach. Fabulous sea and mountain views, pleasant pool, and fresh bedrooms. Dining options include an oyster bar. 140 rooms.

Villa Turística Santo Domingo ✪ *Santo Domingo; Bartolomé Masó; Tel. (023) 595180.* Memorably remote Sierra Maestra base south of Bartolomé Masó. 20 simple huts under towering mountains, amid an orchid garden and next to a river. Walking expeditions offered.

SANTIAGO DE CUBA

Cubanacán Santiago de Cuba ✪✪✪✪ *Avenida de las Américas y Calle M; Tel. (0226) 42656/42612; fax (0226) 41756.* A post-modernist, multicoloured tower block, this is Cuba's most ostentatious hotel. Six bars (one with spectacular views from the rooftop), a luxurious pool, indulgent buffets, a snazzy nightclub, obsequious staff. 3 km (2 miles) from the city centre. 302 rooms.

Villa Gaviota Santiago ✪–✪✪ *Avenida Manduley No. 502 e/ 19 y 21; Vista Alegre; Tel. (0226) 41368/41346.* 4 km (2½ miles) from the city centre in a peaceful, leafy suburb, this hotel has a lovely secluded pool and good, roomy accommodation (especially superior rooms) scattered through old villas. 50 rooms.

PARQUE BACONAO

Club Amigo Bucanero ✪✪ *Arroyo La Costa Km 4; Tel. (022) 27126/28130.* Facing a rocky shoreline and with its own picturesque sandy cove, this isolated, low-rise, well-maintained hotel complex has 200 rustic-style rooms.

LTI Carisol Resort Hotel ✪✪ *Carretera Baconao, Km 10, Playa Cazonal; Tel. (022) 8519/7601.* A German-managed hotel in a picturesque setting at the eastern end of the park. Bungalows and mini villas spaciously arranged among open gardens. Good pool, slightly scruffy beach but with an opportunity to swim alongside tame dolphins. 164 rooms.

Cubanacán La Gran Piedra ✪ *Carretera La Gran Piedra, Km 14; Tel. (022) 5913.* Beneath the summit of La Gran Piedra, 22 bungalows and suites with sitting-rooms, kitchenettes, and amazing views. No pool.

GUANTÁNAMO

Guantánamo ✪ *Calle 13 Norte e/ Ahogado y 1 Oeste; Tel. (021) 326015/324444.* A poor, Soviet-style hotel, but the only accommodation for foreigners for miles around, and departure point for trips to view the American naval base (see page 80). 124 rooms.

BARACOA

Hotel Horizonte El Castillo ✪ *Calixto García; Loma del Paraiso; Tel. (021) 42103/42125/42147.* One of Cuba's most charming hotels, converted from one of Baracoa's old forts. Wonderful pool, magical views, helpful staff, and 20 spacious bedrooms. Delicious coconut-flavoured food.

Recommended Restaurants

As a general rule, the food served in hotels is better quality than anywhere else on the island. If you're feeling under-nourished, a buffet (always available to non-residents) in a luxury hotel is usually a good bet.

Restaurants can be hilariously overstaffed, service can be frustratingly slow, and the menu often bears little relation to what's really available. Yet dining out has its pleasures: the setting is often a fine colonial courtyard, the seafood can be very tasty, and in modest restaurants you may be eating with Cubans.

Arrive at restaurants by 8:00 p.m. or earlier, as food can run out later. Reservations are not necessary except at the very busiest times of year. However, if you're travelling far, check opening hours in advance: many tourist-oriented restaurants outside the resorts, Havana and Santiago usually open only in the daytime.

The price bands below indicate the cost of a three-course meal in U.S. dollars, excluding drinks, tips, and shellfish, which, though inexpensive by international standards, is always far and away the priciest dish on the menu. Only rely on restaurants in top hotels taking credit cards (see page 119), and even then remember that American credit cards are not accepted. Foreigners find it virtually impossible to pay for meals in pesos (see page 118).

✪	under $12
✪✪	$12–25
✪✪✪	over $25

OLD HAVANA

La Bodeguita del Medio ✪✪ *Empredado No. 207 e/ San Ignacio y Cuba; Tel. (07) 624498/618442.* Now into its sixth decade, this scruffy, graffiti-scrawled den has played host to countless celebrities, many of whom, from Frank Sinatra to

Salvadore Allende, have left their mark on the walls. Hemingway liked to drink his mojitos here, and now a constant stream of tourists use them to wash down good Creole cuisine. Pork dishes are the house speciality.

Café Paris ✪ *San Ignacio No. 202 esq. Obispo.* An airy, 24-hour café with lively music — a popular choice with Cubans and tourists alike. Drinks and inexpensive snacks like chicken and crisps and sandwiches.

Divina Pastora ✪✪ *Fortaleza de la Cabaña; Tel. (07) 623886.* Take the tunnel under the harbour to reach this stylish restaurant, set in a beautifully converted old battery by the waterside below the fort. Good fish dishes and correct, swift service.

El Floridita ✪✪✪ *Monserrate No. 557 esq. Obispo; Tel. (07) 631063.* The classiest and most expensive bar and restaurant in town. The rather grand muralled dining-room serves expensive and sometimes memorable seafood. (See page 34)

Don Giovanni ✪ *Tacón No. 4 esq. Empedrado; Tel. (07) 335979.* Simple Italian fare (a better choice for a snack than for a full meal) in the courtyard of a classic blue-and-white colonial mansion. Popular with Cubans, good live music.

Al Medina ✪ *Oficios No. 12 e/ Obispo y Obrapía; Tel. (07) 630862.* Tucked away at the back of the Casa de los Árabe's lovely courtyard. Middle Eastern cooking intermingled with traditional Cuban dishes. Closes around 8:00 p.m. daily.

El Patio ✪✪ *Plaza de la Catedral; Tel. (07) 338146;* One of the most sumptuous, romantic settings for a meal, in what is arguably Havana's most splendidly painted and restored colonial courtyard. A good-value, set Creole meal as well as more imaginative fare. The very popular drinks terrace looks on to the Plaza de la Catedral.

El Patio Colonial ✪ *Plaza de Armas;* A touristy, outdoor café serving pizzas, sandwiches and ice creams, as well as plates of Creole food and cocktails.

Sevilla ✪–✪✪✪ *Trocadero e/ Zulueta y Prado; Tel. (07) 338580.* The Old Havana hotel boasts a splendid main restaurant with a stuccoed rooftop, as well as a pretty, tiled Spanish restaurant, and stylish cafeteria.

La Torre de Marfil ✪ *Mercaderes e/ Obispo y Obrapía; Tel. (07) 623466.* An odd combination of Chinese waiters, music, and food in a handsome old colonial building. Good-value set meals.

La Zaragozana ✪✪ *Monserrate No. 352 e/ Obispo y Obrapía; Tel.(07) 631062.* Next to El Floridita, a rustic-style restaurant with reliably tasty fish dishes. Solicitous service.

NEW HAVANA

Don Agamenón ✪✪ *Calle 17 No. 60 e/ M y N; Vedado.* A Neoclassical villa stylishly decorated with modern art and wicker furniture, and serving traditional Cuban cuisine with chicken specialities. Also an open-air bar with a barbeque.

La Cecilia ✪✪✪ *Avenida 5 e/ 110 y 112; Miramar; Tel. (07) 331562* Large, plush restaurant with good international cuisine in a lovely garden full of palms and jagüey trees. Cabaret show at 9:30 p.m. Thursday to Sunday.

1830 ✪✪ *Malecón e/ 20 y 22; Vedado; Tel. (07) 34504.* Old seaside villa with faded, chandeliered rooms, situated at the western end of Vedado. Eclectic cuisine, with the emphasis primarily on fish.

Nacional de Cuba ✪–✪✪✪ *Calle O esq. 21; Vedado; Tel. (07) 333564/333567.* With a stunning chandeliered dining-room for à la carte meals, excellent buffet dinners, and substantial snacks (chicken, burgers, etc.) also available in the efficient cafeteria, the dining options in this grand hotel (see page 131) are nearly always guaranteed to revivify flagging systems.

El Rápido ✪ *Línea e/ L y M; Vedado.* This somewhat unusual 24-hour drive-in, fast-food burger joint, is staffed by waitresses decked out in denim jackets serving Cubans in their Cadillacs. There is also a sit-down café.

COJÍMAR

La Terraza ✪✪ *Calle Real y Candelaria; Tel. 653471.* Founded in 1925, this a charming waterside fish restaurant was once frequented by Hemingway and is now covered in evocative photos of the writer.

VARADERO

Las Américas ✪✪✪ *Avenida Las Américas, Mansión Dupont; Tel. (05) 337013.* Grand seaside mansion serving adventurous dishes — beef with brie, chicken with coconut — with variable success. Lunchtime snacks also available on the terrace.

Internacional ✪✪ *Carretera Las Américas; Tel. (05) 667038.* The hotel's buffet dinners are the best in the resort and good value, with stunning spreads.

Kiki's Club ✪–✪✪ *Avenida 1 and Calle; 5.* Informal bistro-cum-bar, serving pasta and good pizzas — try one topped with lemon or crayfish.

El Mesón del Quijote ✪✪–✪✪✪ *Carretera Las Américas Tel. (05) 62975* Look for the floodlit knight and his steed towards the eastern end of the resort. Quasi-Spanish cuisine in a pretty, candlelit dining-room, with good live music.

Parque Josone ✪–✪✪✪
A clutch of themed restaurants lie around the park. The menuless La Casa de Antigüedades (✪✪✪, tel. 62044), with beautifully furnished, intimate candlelit dining-rooms, does not offer a menu butspecializes in shellfish and steak. The lakeside Dante (✪✪, tel. 63306) is a small, serious trattoria, while La Campana (✪–✪, tel. 63306) serves inexpensive creole food in a pleasant, rustic environment.

CIENFUEGOS

Palacio del Valle ✪✪ *Calle 37 esq. 2; Punta Gorda; Tel. (0432) 6366.* Next to the Hotel Jagua, this ornate Moorish palace (see page 60) has a ground-floor restaurant serving reasonable seafood (including lobster offered in no less than half a dozen ways, and paella), and a rooftop bar.

TRINIDAD

La Canchánchara ✪ *Rubén M. Villena e/ P. Guinart y C. Redondo;* A bar in a leafy courtyard, named after a drink which combines aguardiente, honey, and lime juice. Spirited live music daily from around 10:30 a.m.-3:00 p.m.

El Jigüe ✪✪ *Ruben M. Villena esq. P. Guinart; Tel. (0419) 4315.* A beautiful, airy colonial house with a gloriously painted facade and terrace leading on to a little square. Chicken specialities. Closes at 5:00 p.m.

Santa Ana ✪✪ *Santo Domingo esq. Santa Ana; Tel. (0419) 3140.* A former prison on the old town's edge, handsomely restored to include a stylish restaurant off its glowing orange courtyard, and a cool bar overlooking the dilapidated Santa Ana church. Open daytime and evening.

CAMAGÜEY

La Campana de Toledo ✪ *Plaza de San Juan de Dios.* A chiming bell welcomes you as you enter one of the city's prettiest courtyards, decorated with tinajones and an old carriage. The specialty of the house is "beef stuffed with Spanish sausage"! Open to 5:00 p.m.

PLAYA SANTA LUCIA

Lobster House ✪✪ *La Boca.* A waterside shack in a ramshackle hamlet by Los Cocos beach serving lobster, shrimp, and crab in a simple but idyllic setting.

GUARDALAVACA

El Ancla ✪✪ *Playa Guardalavaca; Tel. (024) 30145.* Seafood platters and pastas and a waterside drinks terrace in a fabulous position at the eastern end of the beach (walk across the beach and river to reach it).

BAYAMO

1513 ✪ *General García esq. Lora; Tel. (024) 425921.* The best restaurant in town offers an insight into local life, as it's packed with Cuban families and bereft of tourists. Hearty, traditional Cuban fare served until 10:00 p.m.

Cuba

MANZANILLO

Las Américas ✪ *Parque Manuel de Céspedes.* Set in the town's main square, this wonderful old colonial building has friendly and welcoming staff, few tourists, and delicious lobsters and steaks at rock-bottom prices. Nevertheless, be prepared to eat early in the evening.

SANTIAGO DE CUBA

Café La Isabelica ✪ *Aguilera y Calvario.* This is a famous coffee bar serving straight, iced, and liqueur coffees and little else. A great place to meet Cubans.

La Claqueta ✪ *Felix Peña e/ Heredia y Bartolomé Masó.* Just off Parque Céspedes, a fun, outdoor, late-night bar with live music, dancing, drinking, and plenty of atmosphere; usually just a smattering of tourists and lots of young Cubans to meet.

El Morro ✪✪ *Carretera del Morro; Tel. (0226) 91576.* In a superb clifftop location on a vine-covered terrace next to El Morro castle (see page 78), this restaurant specializes in horsemeat but also offers conventional Creole fare.

1900 ✪✪ *Bartolomé Masó No. 354; e/ Hartmann y Pío Rosado; Tel. (0226) 23507.* The Creole food isn't great, but the mansion's courtyard with its lilied fountain and two flower-bedecked drinks terraces upstairs more than compensate.

Tocororo ✪✪✪ *Avenida Manduley No. 57 esq. 7; Vista Alegre; Tel. (0226) 43761.* As close as Cuba gets to nouvelle cuisine, with a lobster and steak combination the speciality (no menus). The setting is a posh villa, with individual, chandeliered dining-rooms.

BARACOA

El Castillo ✪✪ *Calixto García; Loma del Paraíso; Tel. (021) 42103/42125/42147.* A very charming restaurant in this excellent hotel (see page 138) offering a selection of delicious coconut-flavoured fish and rice dishes, as well as the local sweet, *cucurucho.*